SOWING
A BETTER
GARDEN

SOWING A BETTER GARDEN

John Kelly

UNWIN

HYMAN

LONDON SYDNEY WELLINGTON

First published in Great Britain by Unwin Hyman,
an imprint of Unwin Hyman Limited, 1988

UNWIN HYMAN LIMITED
15–17 Broadwick Street,
London W1V 1FP

Allen & Unwin Australia Pty Ltd,
8 Napier Street,
North Sydney, NSW 2060,
Australia

Allen & Unwin with the Port Nicholson Press,
60 Cambridge Terrace,
Wellington,
New Zealand

British Library Cataloguing in Publication Data

Kelly, John
    Sowing a better garden
    I. Gardens. Plants. Propogation from
    seeds
    I. Title
    635'.0431

ISBN 0–04–440222–8

Designed by Julian Holland
Typeset by Latimer Trend & Company Ltd, Plymouth
Printed in Portugal by
Printer Portuguesa,

Contents

To own a bit of ground, to scratch it with a hoe,
to plant seeds, and watch their renewal of life,—
this is the commonest delight of the race, the most
satisfactory thing a man can do.

CHARLES DUDLEY WARNER.
My Summer in a Garden (1871)

We plough the fields and scatter
The good seed on the land,
But it is fed and watered
By God's Almighty Hand.

JAMES MONTGOMERY CAMPBELL
(1817–1878)

Some seeds fell by the way side.

MATTHEW 13:4

The author wishes to thank
Tony Bates, who took the majority
of the photographs and, also
Connie Austen Smith, who started the idea

and to dedicate this book to
Alec Duguid, who started the author gardening

and Freda Howitt, who started the author.

Foreword

Seed science is extremely complex, and in writing a book for gardeners I have often simplified matters to a degree which seed scientists may well find overdone.

I have not gone into the differences between endospermic and non-endospermic seeds, nor have I dwelt on the different kinds of immature or rudimentary embryos. Treatments with giberillic acid, sulphuric acid, and potassium nitrate are not procedures that home gardeners are likely to attempt; neither are they going to have the facilities for subjecting seeds of various species to the wide ranges of temperatures that optimum germination requires.

The gardener who wishes to become more sympathetic with his plants will not have his cause advanced by being lectured upon the role of oxygen in chemical changes in the seed after imbibition, or upon the little-understood formation of enzyme systems. What will assist him will be a truly empathetic approach—one in which 'thinking like a plant' is the aim.

All non-fiction writers aspire to tell the truth. In gardening there is often a discrepancy between scientific truth and the kind which can be ascribed to common sense. For example, I have appeared to dismiss the growing of annuals as 'easy'. Scientifically this is not really true, as annual seeds show tendencies towards dormancy unless dry-stored for six months or so. In common sense (gardening) terms it is so, as annual seed is, in practice, always given this period of storage.

I am, of course, not a seed scientist. Indeed, I am not a scientist of any kind, just a gardener whose lot it has been to sow innumerable batches of seed of all kinds of plants over a long period of my life. This book is based on experience, both my own and that of respected colleagues. What that experience and the work of the scientists has to teach above all is that there is a great deal left to be learned.

JOHN KELLY
ABBOTSBURY, DORSET
1988

A Note on Gender

In referring to types of gardeners I have used the masculine form throughout.

This is intended to be inclusive, as in the term 'mankind'. It is most certainly not used exclusively.

Women form a large proportion of the best gardeners in the world. They are less boastful, more caring, and generally have better taste than men. They tend to love their plants dearly, while at the same time retaining sufficient realism to enable them to view the plant world as one consisting of entities with limited life-spans.

Those who resent the yoke which the female sex has worn for centuries (and still to a large extent wears) are asked to forgive an author for whom it would be an obstacle to fluency continually to have to refer to he/she and him/her.

The author is male, but his respect for his fellow gardeners makes no distinction as to gender. It is earned by those who know that one lifetime is enough merely to graduate from the kindergarten class in the school whose head teacher is Nature.

Introduction

Why Grow from Seed?

For most gardeners, sowing seed means an annual round of repetition. They will consult the same two or three seed catalogues that their parents before them did, and they will follow much the same pattern in their choice that they have done for years.

Their selections are likely to be confined to vegetables and annuals, with a few biennials thrown in for good measure. Cabbage 'Harbinger' will be duly set in autumn, with 'Christmas Drumhead' following it in the spring. Gallons of 'Early Nantes' carrot seed will be deposited on the lighter soils of the country when the sun has warmed them, while millions of the lettuce 'Webbs Wonderful' are started on their way to flopping gracelessly amid the mayonnaise. Floods of white alyssum, scarlet salvia, and blue lobelia will soon stand in regiments throughout the land, as if to say that patriotism comes and goes with the summer.

No person, however, who sets his hand to the soil should ever be the butt of sneering or mockery. That first step on to the land is a commitment to an activity which is an art. It would be as cruel to castigate a gardener for his limitations as it would be to scorn the first crayonings of a bright child in whom lie the embryo talents of a Constable or a Turner.

The world of the seeds of plants is vast and, like that of painting, infinitely explorable. No lifetime is long enough for its variety to pall, and age serves only to enhance the childish joy which greets the emergence of something new. The germination of one's annual crop of petunias may well engender a measure of satisfaction, but the appearance of a rarity from some far-off uninhabited hill can create a deep-seated pleasure that is made pure by its simplicity.

To live with a plant from its sowing to its maturity is, too, a deeply fulfilling experience. To buy a plant, nurture it, and see it grow to full-flowering adulthood is to gain a great deal, but to have handled the seed is to have touched creation. A great Scottish plantsman, approaching his old age, once showed me his garden on a sunny spring day. When we reached a glade in his wood, he stopped and silently gazed on the brilliant mounds of dwarf rhododendrons that decorated it. Soft pinks, brilliant reds and shimmering whites spread like an opulent carpet towards the dark pines, while candelabra primulas danced in the breeze beside the stream. 'Isn't it wonderful to think,' he said eventually, 'that this was once a few seeds in my pocket.'

The Limited Gardener

Such peaceful euphoria cannot be bought. This is not only because to buy plants is to relinquish their birth and childhood; it is also because the range of plants that are offered for sale is limited, and because by sticking to this quite narrow selection, one remains a limited gardener.

In days gone by, a nurseryman would often grow things because he liked them and he would, more often than not, have a few extra plants tucked away for sale to people whom he favoured. He might, too, be persuaded to raise a special item for a good customer as a special order, and he would usually be too much of a plantsman to resist growing many good plants that were uneconomical. Plants that took many years to reach saleable size, or those that required great pains in their propagation, could be found at a reasonable price, while some, whose seed provided poor germination rates, or whose cuttings gave a low strike rate, would present him with an irresistible challenge. Such craftsmen, whose livings were made on a balance of the profitable and the loss-making, are now as rare as some of their stocks. The advent of the large garden centre and modern economics has changed horticulture beyond recognition. Most garden centres buy in a large proportion of the plants they sell. Often their wholesale suppliers are themselves supplied in part by contract growers. Margins shrink, and profits are made by large-scale selling; turnover and movement of stocks are the keys to commercial survival. To obey the law of supply and demand is the route to success.

Nurseries today must supply what there is the greatest demand for, and the demand from customers becomes concentrated upon that of which there is the greatest supply. There is little time for the nurseryman to educate his customers and suggest this and that plant that might be a little different, so the gardener finds comfort in sales beds filled with names that he knows. Plants that can be propagated in thousands with relative ease in factory conditions form a litany of modern gardening—berberis, cotoneaster, clematis, conifers . . .

Of course, like almost everything in life, the history of nursery practice has its weak spot into which the cynic may thrust his lance. The ownership of houses with gardens upon which money could be spent has not always been the prerogative of the working man and woman. A few decades ago, the nurseryman found his trade among the relative few with the means to indulge their pastime, and prices reflected this. A man could cheerfully indulge a customer with a plant for five shillings that had cost him six to produce if the dozen other plants had only cost him sixpence. When the average working wage was three pounds a week, how many could afford to furnish their gardens with bought plants?

No wonder the cottage garden with its seed-grown flowers and vegetables was so popular!

The prices of plants were able to remain stable until quite recently—and why not, with such margins to be soaked up? Now, however, the producer's costs have gone through the roof and thus the prices of plants have rocketed. We think twice about furnishing our gardens with bought plants and, once again, our thoughts go to seed-sown gardens, while the big growers wonder where it will all end.

Tender Plants

No matter where you garden, your local climate will tend to limit the range of plants that you can grow. Climates, however, are not sharply delineated; they have fuzzy edges, providing areas at the margins within which experiments can be carried out.

It is, however, an expensive proposition to go out and buy a plant in order to see if it will survive in conditions beyond those for which nature designed it. My own experience in running a large garden in a climatically unique part of England suggests that fifty per cent of the plants that can reasonably be tried out beyond the accepted levels of hardiness will die within the first five years. Of those that survive, ten per cent will be killed when a freak winter comes along.

Taking an optimistic fifty per cent survival rate in the long term, one is facing a substantial loss if one goes out and buys the plants. On the other hand, to grow them from seed costs very little, and if only half of a large number of plants survive, the garden soon becomes a very interesting one.

To take *Eucalyptus* as an example is reasonable, as I know that two species *E. gunnii* and *E. johnstonii* are hardy with me no matter what the winter. By hardy here I mean plants that suffer no appreciable damage to their foliage. I have tried forty species out of doors and have totally lost half of them. Of the others, besides the two above species, *EE. nitens, pauciflora, parvifolia, dalrympleana* and *viminalis* have emerged undamaged from the lowest temperatures this century. Ten other species have suffered damage ranging from bad to severe, but have all survived and produced new shoots either from the trunks or from the bases.

Were I to have bought all forty, I should have suffered an unacceptable financial loss and it would be very expensive to replace the plants. As I grew them from seed, however, and can obtain seed again, the loss is more emotional than anything else, and the gain in knowledge has been considerable.

It is interesting that one of the eucalypts to succumb was *E. niphophila*, the Snow Gum. This is one of the very hardiest, but mine came very close to death while another tree in the much colder midlands of England was untouched. This is an example of the phenomenon of provenance, a term used to describe the source of seed within the geographical distribution of a species. *Eucalyptus* species often range over territory which may include mountains where there is much frost and plains where there is little or none. It is obviously important to obtain seed with as cold a provenance as possible, and I do this by writing nice letters to kind people in Australia, although in this case my friend in the midlands must have written a nicer one.

In citing *Eucalyptus nitens* as one of the unsullied survivors I have been less than frank. The Shining Gum, with its large, blue-green, sickle-shaped leaves and glistening white trunk, is represented by two specimens. One is perfectly all right, but the other has just managed to come through and has made shoots from the lower two-thirds of the trunk, from which I have encouraged a new branch structure to form. They are from the same batch of seed and are planted about 15ft (5m) from one another. Why one should emerge from severe conditions so much better than the other is unknown to me, but the point is that I was able to plant out more than one because I grew them from seed and had the plants to use. Had I sold them, one of my customers would have been much happier than the other.

Growing tender, or marginally tender plants from seed allows you to try them in different parts of the garden. It also permits you to learn a great deal more about plants in general, it helps you to understand the problem of hardiness in plants (although nobody will ever fully comprehend it) and it makes it possible for your garden to be a far more interesting place than it would be if you stuck with the ironclads of the garden centre.

Many plants from outside the cool temperate regions grow rather quickly. With some eucalypts making up to 6ft (2m) of growth in a year, there is no great problem in replacing those that have died. Although I confess to a great sense of loss in losing a 40ft (13m) specimen of *Acacia dealbata*, the 'mimosa' of florists, to frost, I am not too heartbroken, as it was only nine years old and it had been a conspicuous tree in flower for four. Trying tender plants can be a continuous, fascinating, and very instructive process, but it is one for the seed-raiser or the millionaire. Of the two, you may be sure which will have the more fun.

Seed Sowing and Tradition

Although growing plants from seed can avoid a great deal of expense, it is by no means the 'cheap' end of gardening.

Perhaps the view that it is derives from times when the ordinary man or woman could only afford to garden if they grew everything from seed. Perhaps too, and with some justification, it is encouraged by the contents of the catalogues of the great seed houses. Once again, the economies of supply and demand come into play and the pages and pages of vegetables, annuals and biennials reflect the interplay of supply, demand, and profit at the margin.

There is absolutely nothing wrong with such catalogues, nor with the gardeners whose needs they serve. It would be a poor world if a person were not able to grow precisely what he wished in his own garden, and annuals should not be looked down upon because of their ease of cultivation. Vegetables, too, are a delight when well-grown, and nothing that the shops can offer can match the freshness of flavour and texture that comes from the garden.

Nevertheless, seed-raising has an aura of poor man's gardening about it, and this is a pity, as it forms the top division of horticultural skill and involves at any one time the most important plants in the whole horticultural scene.

Were it not for those who germinated the seed sent back to home countries by the great plant collectors, our gardens would be completely unrecognizable. The great wealth of China and the Himalayas, the exotica of Chile and the Andes, and the tricky rarities of Iran and the Hindu Kush would be unknown to us, save as herbarium specimens, had not supreme craftsmanship been brought to bear in the collecting, storing, cleaning, sowing and growing-on of what has become our garden plant heritage.

The process continues as we find ourselves once more in an age of great plant collectors. A steady stream of new introductions is reaching our gardens from all over the world and much of it is arriving in the postal deliveries of amateur gardeners who have cut their teeth on less rarified material.

The plant health regulations that govern the transfer of plant material other than seeds between countries are now so strict (and strictly enforced) that seed is effectively the only means of transporting plants across the world without many losses and a great deal of cost and trouble. Modern air travel has taken away the risk of short-lived seeds perishing en route, and so a great international traffic has arisen between gardeners, often involving plants that are rare or that are not grown at all in the countries of the recipients.

What with the great strides being made in new plants from such sources, the new opportunities afforded to amateur plant breeders, and the decline of the variety offered by the nursery industry, so far from being the poor end of the gardening spectrum, seed-raising has become the very top drawer of horticulture.

Cultivars

Of course, not all garden plants can be grown from seed. Whereas all species *can* be raised from seed in gardens, provided that viable seed can be obtained from some source and provided that the right conditions are provided, cultivars cannot, in as much as they will not breed true.

A cultivar is a form, or variety of a species or hybrid that has been propagated vegetatively (by some method such as cuttings) and given a name—such as *Camellia japonica* 'Giulio Nuccio'. This brilliant red, semi-double camellia, with a boss of golden stamens in the centre of the flower and a hint of 'fish tail' in its leaf, will set seed readily in a favourable season, the seed-pods appearing like brown crab-apples late in the year.

The seed will certainly germinate, although it may take its time about it. What is equally certain, though, is that you could go on sowing seed from 'Giulio Nuccio' for ever and a day and you would never once raise a plant that was the same as the parent. Indeed, the chances of obtaining a really good camellia from a few dozen seeds would be slight, to say the least.

As we shall see, though, some of the greatest fun is to be had from having a go and trying to raise a worthwhile new cultivar, but the only way to obtain plants of a given one is by means of vegetative propagation.

If a friend gives you two cuttings of a cultivar, you have a fairly good chance of ending up with two plants, but with a pinch of seed from a species, you are almost certain to derive many more than that.

Gardening has a great deal to do with taste. It is, in this as in so many fields, rather invidious to speak of 'good' and 'bad' taste, and a sense of historical perspective tends to lead one to the conclusion that today's good taste is probably tomorrow's bad. Not only that; it is also arguable that 'good' taste is manufactured by a few, who immediately change it once it becomes universally accepted.

The flight from bright colours in flowers to a strict regime involving a restricted, flabby palette of 'tasteful' pastels and pinks is just such a trend in the gardening world. Those who have not the slightest interest in being 'in' will soon find that the wheel has come full circle when their flamboyant reds and oranges become tomorrow's high fashion. Meanwhile, where does true discrimination lie, as opposed to mere fad?

Probably in a preference for species rather than cultivars, although this should not in itself become a dictum of the pace-setters. If a man wishes to fill his garden with show dahlias, their perfect, enormous blooms each protected by its paper bag, then let him, and allow him the respect his great skill deserves, but if a small voice whispers that you really prefer the delicacy of species to the vulgarity of so many cultivars, then listen, because your taste is for nature, and your skill will involve nature's method of propagation.

Species have, undeniably, an airiness and elegance that becomes lost when the search for size and complication of bloom takes over. Much plant breeding leads inexorably towards the overstated and the grotesque, where the essential balance between the structure of the plant and of its flowers is, to a greater or lesser degree, upset.

The rhododendron fan who grows the Hardy Hybrids, whose massive, stiff trusses swank their tarty ostentation for a short season before lapsing into unrelieved torpor for almost the whole year, will reap far greater reward by patiently awaiting the maturity of the species, whose whole appearance is as lastingly beautiful and distinguished as that of overbred hybrids is coarse and uncouth.

He may be able to buy plants of species rhododendrons from a very few nurseries, but they will cost a great deal and will probably have to come from far afield. With the contents of a few seed-packets and the willingness to wait, he can explore the whole world of one of the most fascinating of genera.

Broadening Horizons

Growing plants from seed is a simple occupation, greatly at variance with the high-flown pursuits with which we encumber ourselves generally. It is a retreat into the real world of nature and towards the quieter virtues of the human psyche. Patience, delicacy and caring are qualities we need to find within ourselves if we are to succeed, as are humility and forbearance. There are no whizz kids among successful seed gardeners, and it is no good shouting 'Not fair!' when failure is encountered.

The limited gardener, shackled heretofore by the stocks of garden centres, will find his knowledge of the plant world expanding at a rate he could never have imagined. His skill will increase greatly as he becomes familiar with his plants from cradle to grave, and his contacts with others of like mind may, in all likelihood, be found all over the world. As a garden planner, too, he will be able to think, not in ones and twos, but in drifts of plants, highlighted by single specimens of architectural impact or by groups of contrasting colour or form. He will have to take longer over things than the instant gardener, but he can learn not to be snobbish about annual flowers as he uses them for effect until his perennials are established.

In a remote and, to many eyes, inhospitable place in the Highlands of Scotland, where a mere twenty-five people inhabit fifty square miles, lives a man who was once a nurseryman in a far more popular and comfortable area. The restrictions upon what economics allowed him to grow, the reams of paperwork, and the sheer monotony drove him to seek release in a spot where the 'garden' was a thin gruel of saturated peat and shale, covered with a wilderness of wild rhododendron and stringy birches.

It is now a heart-stopping oasis of startling beauty. He has not tamed the poor, boggy soil, but has experimented with many thousands of kinds of plants, losing a large proportion of them in his search for those that would thrive, but encouraging and nurturing those that could adapt.

He is quiet and deeply content, and his greatest pride is that he created his extraordinary garden, not from the beds of a nursery, but from packets of seed.

Seeds and Germination

What is a Seed?

The animal and plant kingdoms work in completely different ways and because we belong to the former, we tend to see things from the animal point of view. This can lead to a lack of understanding of plants, especially when short, scientific definitions are given.

A seed is an embryo plant. This is true, but in the animal kingdom, embryos are looked after assiduously by their parents for the most part (fish and amphibians tend to be exceptional), and they are cared for and protected for the early parts of their lives. In the plant world, on the other hand, embryos are cast out, sometimes very forcibly, by their parents, to thrive or die in the cold, hard world as best they may.

The embryo plant—not yet having attained babyhood—may fly for several miles, or take an ocean journey lasting for months. It may pass through fire or the intestines of a bird or other animal, or it may lie buried in the ground for decades. Some embryos will die if they do not reach a suitable place for further development within a very few weeks, while others may wander the face of the globe for many years intact before finding a resting place.

Usually, but not always, the embryo is equipped with a degree of protection, a small food supply, and sometimes with the means of propulsion through air or water. It is as if the parent plant had issued all its embryos with short-term life-support systems and then cast them adrift. Indeed, our understanding of seeds and of their germination is aided by thinking of the seed as a life-capsule.

Some plants are more generous than others in providing these aids. Orchids, for example, give out no food reserves to their progeny, whose embryos may have not much more than one hundred cells in their makeup. Where this happens, though, such vast numbers of seeds are produced that the chances of a few germinating are quite high, and only a few are needed to keep the species going. On the other hand, very large life-capsules indeed—ocean liners rather than liferafts—can be seen sailing in the Indian Ocean, where the Double Coconut reaches sizes up to 18in (45cm) long. A dozen or so of these give a very good chance that one or two will find good conditions in time for germinating—compare this with one to four million from a seed capsule of an orchid!

An embryo plant is a soft and delicate structure which

needs some sort of armour against the outside world if it is to stand much chance. The prolific orchids do not bother too much, but most seeds are provided with a coat of relatively hard material. This is usually double, the outer part being the harder, and it has a tiny pore in it just opposite the tip of the radicle, the embryo root.

The armour may be augmented by structures other than the true seed-coat, but it all adds up to a tough, durable protection and often has devices built into it that facilitate travel.

The whole point of the dispersal of seeds and of the need for providing protection while they are on the journeys is because there is not much point in germination happening too close to the immoveable parents. The mobile members of the animal kingdom do not have to overcome the problem of their offspring having to share the identical space and food-supply, but plants must ensure that their progeny can find a place where they can develop to maturity unencumbered. Once germination takes place it is too late; the embryo's travels are over for ever.

Furthermore, if circumstances change—if there is a landslide, an incursion of salt water or, most importantly, a change of climate, the species must have a chance of moving to somewhere more favourable if it is to survive. Great changes, like the Ice Ages and their disappearance, have seen species travel great distances, and it is seed dispersal that has enabled them to do so.

Preserving the Species

Sometimes it seems as if gardening is to botany what seventeenth-century medicine was to modern clinical practice. Doctors used to diagnose, prescribe and advise without the slightest basis in science but with a strong underlying mythology. Similarly, gardeners employ a largely 'chuck it and chance it' approach, which involves doing things for no better reason than that their fathers and grandfathers did it, or because something worked once by chance and they reckon that it will always work.

In no field is this eccentric empiricism more profoundly demonstrated than in dealing with seed. Modern gardeners are often highly educated and go to great lengths to understand other things fully. They may have encyclopaedic knowledge of the anatomy of their motor vehicles, deep, hard-won understanding of canine psychology or of the intricacies of plumbing, but set them among plants and it is as if their ideas had become set in amber some long time ago in history.

While it is true that there is something of a miracle that occurs every time that a seed germinates, this is not to say that it is a miraculous event. In nature there is a reason for everything, and in everything there is reason to be found. When seeds refuse to germinate, it is not because of some malevolent or spiteful spirit that lurks within them or in the mythosphere that surrounds the gardener; it is because something real has either gone wrong or has failed to be understood.

The key to understanding seeds and their behaviour is, once it is appreciated what a seed is, to comprehend the purpose of seed production and dispersal.

An individual plant is of no interest to Nature. She is totally collectivist in her philosophy and is concerned only with the benefit of the species. She manufactures her beauty merely with the eye of the beholder in view and is completely totalitarian. The fact that we find flowers beautiful is a by-product of the system; it is the pollinators that count, and it is to them that the display is projected. To think that flowers are produced for our benefit is to be anthropocentric. It is we who have evolved a pleasure in flowers; flowers have not evolved for our pleasure.

A plant is a member of a species and it exists only to preserve the species. Its vegetative parts are there for food production and anchorage and to act as scaffolding upon which the reproductive parts are displayed to the pollinators to the best advantage. Those organs have developed to the optimum degree for attracting the best and most efficient pollinators in the greatest possible numbers.

Androsace glacialis is an exquisitely beautiful cushion plant that grows at high altitudes in the European Alps. Its habitat is the moraine at the bases of glaciers or at the edges of shallow, slow-moving mountain trickles. When you come across it, its bright floral display, low down to the ground, attracts you irresistibly from the dry path, and you find that its flowers, large for its tiny foliage, are a mixture of white ones and some that are of a very pretty rose-pink.

What happens is that the plant is showing an adaptation to extracting the greatest efficiency from the flies that pollinate it. It is too high up for those insects that might be attracted by coloured flowers with patterns that only their vision can pick out, but its white flowers are attractive to flies. Even so, at these heights there are not all that many flies, so each one that comes by must be encouraged to do its stuff and not to waste time. As soon as a flower has been fertilized, it turns pink, so that the next fly that comes along will turn its attention to a white, unfertilized flower.

The characteristic of having flowers in two colours, which we find so lovely in this species, is merely an instance of the down-to-earth practicality that is nature all over. Reproduce at all costs is the order of the day.

In the Norwegian mountains the season is extremely

short. There is no time for plants to wave their flowers about, languidly posturing like Scarlett O'Hara. *Ranunculus glacialis*, a buttercup that grows on the Finsteraarhorn, will flower in five days from emerging from the snow and mature its seed seventeen days afterwards. Reproduce and get on with it is the whole of the law.

Flowers are merely devices for showing-off the reproductive organs of the plant. Of course, plants that are fertilized by the wind have no need for such vanities; there is no future in displaying to the wind—you might as well as talk to yourself.

Once fertilization has taken place and the seeds have matured, parts of the flower, sometimes their stems, and often the wind itself, are called upon to play their parts in the next phase of the preservation of the species.

It is now the destiny of the plant to ensure that its seeds are dispersed so that a large enough number of them will stand a good chance of finding places that will not only be ideal for germination but also as good as possible for subsequent growth. Many of the methods used make life very difficult for the gardener, as he may well find that those seeds which he wishes to harvest are shot away to where he cannot find them, while those he does not wish to harbour in his garden arrive willy-nilly, borne on the winds, on the feet of birds, or even on his own coat.

That many of these will be weeds speaks only of the great success of those plants that we call weeds. They are so well adapted to a variety of environments that they find congenial homes with the greatest of ease. Annual weeds die after seed-dispersal, and why not? Their lives are of no further use in species which produce vast amounts of unfussy seed. Garden annuals, too, are of little interest to Nature once they have reproduced—their seeds tend to be easygoing, too, and that is why there is not a lot of art in sowing them. It is rather difficult to give them conditions that will not allow them to germinate unless you try really hard.

Make the mistake of cutting weeds back, rather than uprooting them, and you will have an even heavier crop of seeds to deal with. Annual plants, too, when cut back before seed has set, will tend to produce a second flowering. Threaten a plant and it will react by trying to reproduce itself before it dies.

This is why nerines, for example, only flower well if they are grown potbound or allowed to make larger clumps in the same piece of ground so that they become crowded. Hippeastrums, too, require short commons if they are to flower. Some shrubs that display reluctance to flower can be made to believe that they are under threat by lifting them and then dropping them back in the same hole. The little bit of root damage does the trick. It used to be said of *Rhododendron thomsonii*, for instance, that what it needed to make it produce its gorgeous, crimson bells was to be taken for a wheelbarrow ride around the garden. Certainly it will not flower until it is quite old unless it is disturbed, whereas a threatened three-footer will oblige handsomely.

That it is the purpose of nature to preserve the species and not to provide us with a display of flowers can be seen in such plants as the poppy. While it may have a life of only a year or two, its seeds can remain dormant in the soil for decades, as was shown when a fantastic display of field poppies erupted from the disturbed land of the Somme after 1916. The seed, in many ways, is the primary stage of the species, although it would be a mistake to follow this argument too far, in the light of those seeds whose viability is short.

Once we have understood what the significance of seed-dispersal is—to obtain the best possible conditions for germination—we can begin to apply a little reason to the conditions that we provide when we want to germinate seeds in our gardens.

We have already seen that most if not all annuals should provide us with little difficulty. They are annuals simply because they are so successful at germinating in a great variety of conditions. Among perennial plants, though, and not least among trees and shrubs, there is a greater degree of fussiness.

An annual does not have to find a habitat that will support it for very long. Furthermore, if its seeds can bide their time or germinate in batches over the years, changing conditions will not endanger the species. A long lived perennial, on the other hand, will not reach maturity and the ability to reproduce unless it germinates in a situation that will support it for many years. Given conditions that do not suit it well, it will not germinate at all. This is why gardeners who have successfully raised annuals over many years find that they cannot achieve good results with trees and shrubs. Their technique is just not good enough, but they will often fail to see why and will fall back on myth and on the recalcitrant spirit of spite that seems to dog their horticultural footsteps.

Germination

The gardener who has appreciated that the whole drive of nature among the flowering plants is to preserve the species will realize that (if one may put it in such a way) the seeds *want* to germinate. There is nothing in the world quite as eager as a seed, given that it has the right conditions in which to achieve its aims. The seed-raiser, if he is to be successful, must try to match the artificial conditions of his garden to the natural ones in which his seeds do best. In order to do this he must often think about the plant whose seeds he is sowing and try to imagine in what way the reproductive imperative will work in a given species.

Is it likely, for instance, that a primula will germinate in the dark? Will it require much or little moisture? He must think himself into the position of a primula and of its offspring. He will have noticed that primulas tend to grow in glades among trees and not directly under them. They tend, also, to prefer rich soils that are moisture-retentive, or poor ones that are sodden. Primulas, too, do not disperse their seeds very far but tend to be content to colonize a welcoming site once they have found one. They are not in any great hurry to move on, although a few seeds will eventually find their way to a new place and start up a community.

If they thrive in poor, wet soils and are happy to stay put, it is indicative of the importance of moisture rather than food as being the thing they need most. Perhaps they grow in glades rather than beneath trees because the trees take up too much moisture from the soil?

Turning now to the seed, the gardener imagines one that has been sent by its parent into a promising place. It will not have much difficulty in knowing that it is wet as long as it can take up moisture quickly enough. Unfortunately, seeds that can do this tend to have short lives. Our gardener will, therefore, want to sow his primula seed as soon after it is ripe as he can, and in as moist a place as possible. However, he will have noticed that the water around the parents is not static, but clear and clean, so he will understand that he must provide good drainage as well as moisture.

Seeds that are adapted to growing in glades and not under trees with dense canopies (although light, dappled shade from birches, for instance, is acceptable) will not fall prey to having their moisture stolen. Primula seeds, there-fore, tend not to germinate in the dark, and are best sown on the surface of the soil and given just a little shade to protect them in case the sun becomes hot before the leaves are on the surrounding trees.

Our gardener will, after thinking all this, make up a very peaty compost, in which he will have mixed a little sharp sand for drainage, and upon the moist surface of which he will sow his primula seed without covering it. He will put his pot or tray in a closed frame to conserve moisture and will never allow the compost to become dry. He will provide a little shade in the form of netting lest the sun beat down too hard, but his frame will not be in a dark, north-facing spot, lest the seeds feel dangerously overshadowed by what seem to them like trees that are too close.

He will, if all goes well and to plan, soon find that he has an abundant germination on his hands, while his pal across the road, who has treated his primulas like alyssum and sown them in a non-thinking way, is cursing the vagaries of nature and is waxing paranoid about bad luck, bad seed, and how it's not fair and he's going to stick to petunias.

Furthermore, by thinking out the primulas' likes and dislikes, the successful gentleman will plant his results in the best possible conditions for growth and will soon be rewarded with considerable surplus in the form of hundreds of self-sown seedlings! It is then a good bet that, being a generous soul, he will give some to his neighbour, in whose garden they will promptly die, thus embittering the poor chap even further and causing him to abandon gardening as a bad job and to take up bowling.

Observation is a great asset in a gardener and can play a significant part in successful seed-sowing. The beautiful *Pulsatilla vulgaris*, the Easter Anemone, or Pasque flower, is a creature of the hills that has become naturalized in a few select places away from its European home. It has soft, feathery leaves and nodding bells of lilac-purple, encased in woolly calyces. Its seeds are wind-dispersed and have long tails so that the streamlined seed and its appendage form a missile whose head becomes embedded in the soil.

When it finds a good spot with the right degree of moisture, the tail instantly reacts to the presence of water by flailing and twisting and acting like a drill, forcing the seed firmly into the soil. The observant gardener, having once seen this, will realize that, unless he can store the seed perfectly dry and at a low temperature, it is unlikely that the seed will germinate the spring after dispersal or collection. The seed is so obviously adapted for quick germination—or at least, for rapid insertion into its favourite environment— that it must be best sown as soon as it is ripe. He will find out that he is right. Pulsatilla seed is very difficult to germinate the following spring, but is very easy when ripe. If you push the seed into the compost and then water it, the tails will twirl about and seedlings will appear very quickly.

For seeds to germinate, they need water, oxygen, the correct temperature, and the right amount of light. Often they will wait until conditions become optimum before they germinate, and a dormant period ensues. Many seeds are adapted to avoid germination as soon as they are ripe—in contrast to the pulsatilla—in order that they do not have to undergo a winter as vulnerable seedlings. This is why it is fairly safe to leave the majority until the spring, although there will be disappointments if you do not know which ones need to be sown in the autumn.

Ligularia przewalskii

1 The seed-head dispersing.

2 An individual seed.

The unexpectedly hardy arum, *Arisaema candidissimum*, usually germinates within three months of spring sowing.

Tender shrubs like *Eucryphia milliganii* can be tried in varying situations when grown from seed.

Eucryphia milliganii is capable of flowering when very young.

Lilies are almost all very easy from spring-sown seeds. *Lilium henryi* flowers late and is easily grown.

Incarvillea delavayi. Incarvillea seed is best sown in autumn. While others may succeed, the author fails dismally with spring sowings.

The Australian bottle-brush, *Callistemon linearis* is extremely easy from spring-sown seed and is suprisingly hardy.

The seed heads of *Allium christophii* last well in floral arrangements. It flowers in late June.

Seed pods of *Incarvillea delavayi* almost past the perfect moment for collection.

Zantedeschia elliottiana is easy from spring-sown seed but is best brought into winter shelter after a summer by the water-side.

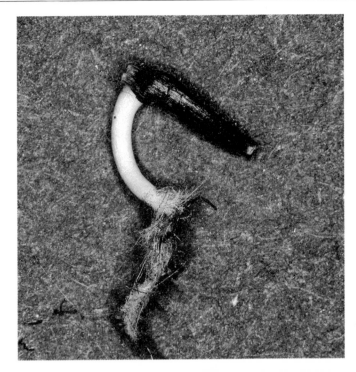

3 Five days after sowing, the root is well developed.

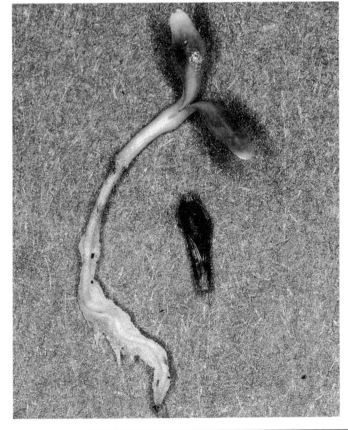

4 The seedling seven days after sowing.

Salvia patens
Stages in the development
of *Salvia patens* from seed
sown in late winter with
bottom heat of 70°F
(21°C).

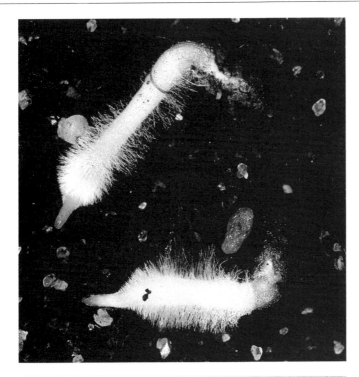

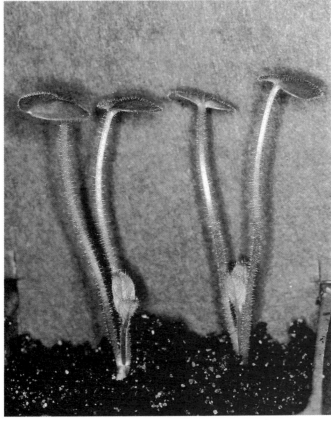

Water

Water content often determines the time when seeds should be sown. Sugar Maple seeds, for instance, die if their water content falls below thirty per cent, and petiolarid primulas react to water loss very rapidly. They must be sown before any desiccation can take place. Even this sort of water content is very low, however, when compared with that of living plants, where it is about ninety per cent, and it is the low water content that damps down activity in seeds and makes them able to lie dormant for long periods.

Seeds are extremely sensitive to water. When they are dry they are in a state of suspended animation, but if they begin to take up water they will either germinate or rot and die. Once the 'trigger' has been sprung the process is irreversible and the seeds become highly vulnerable, whereas previously they were fairly safe. The water content of most seeds is around fifteen per cent, although some tree seeds survive when almost completely dried out, sometimes to less than one per cent.

It is quite a staggering thought that something as simple as the presence or absence of water can make such a vast difference in the life-cycle of a plant. That seeds, buried for several thousand years in the frozen soil of the Arctic should germinate within a couple of weeks after being sown in moist soil is almost beyond belief, and yet it is so. While it is estimated that the longest-lived thing in creation is the Bristle-Cone Pine, it is arguable that it is, in fact, a seed, matured on a plant that has been dead for more than ten thousand years, and still waiting to burst into what would be the shortest phase of its life. It is the species that matters and not the individual; the important thing is the next generation of seed and perhaps another ten thousand years.

Water is absorbed through the seed-coat, and especially by the pore near the radicle, which is called the micropyle. Once this happens, the processes of germination must continue or the seed dies. Enzymes begin to act on the food reserve, which begins to move around in 'packets' to the various points where the most energy is needed. If the supply of water ceases, the process stops and cannot be started again. The essential nature of the steady maintenance of good germination conditions cannot be overemphasized, because it is at this and the next stage that a huge number of seeds are lost in cultivation.

Next, the embryo starts to expand. This is due partly to the absorption of water, when the moisture content of the seed may rise by as much as six hundred per cent or even more, and partly because of growth. Pressure on the seed-coat causes it to rupture, releasing the radicle to search for the soil and the cotyledons (the seed-leaves) to climb towards the light.

Once the radicle has started to function as a root and has penetrated a distance into the soil, the young plant can stand some variation in its water supply and is, above all, no longer in danger from atmospheric dryness, as it can withdraw water from the soil to make up for what it loses from its leaves.

It is worth digressing for a moment at this point in order to clarify the Golden Rule that governs the life of plants. This states that water lost by the leaf must never exceed that gained by the root. This is why plants that are moved from place to place should always have a portion of their upper growth removed—it compensates for root damage that may have occurred—and is also the reason for our putting plastic bags over our cuttings or rooting them under mist. A plant that has no roots, like a cutting, cannot fend for itself in obtaining water and it must be given a constant, artificial supply or its leaves must be prevented from losing water. A germinating seed, too, is a plant without roots, and is exceedingly vulnerable.

This vulnerability is greater in some seeds than in others, but the gardener is well advised to think of it as being at its maximum no matter what he is sowing. This will, above all, make him think of the environment from the seed's point of view, and the depth of understanding of plants and plant habitats that he will acquire by means of this thought will be very large indeed. Rather like the successful angler, who soon learns the advantages of 'thinking like a fish', the gardener who has the best record of germination of the widest range of plants will have learned to 'think like a seed'.

Oxygen

Life on earth is oxygen-based, so it is useless to try to encourage something to live in the absence of air containing oxygen. The growth of the embryo can only take place in the presence of well-oxygenated air, and a compost or soil that is saturated with water or is dense and sticky will be airless and will not allow germination to take place.

All gardeners have at some time in their lives come up against the conundrum of a 'well drained, but moisture-retentive soil'. Nevertheless, no matter how contradictory it may seem, such a soil is not only ideal but is essential to seed-germination.

As a compost is watered, it will initially become soaked so that the spaces between the soil particles become full of water and the air is driven out. Because of the presence of soil microorganisms, this air will have contained quite a high level of carbon dioxide and consequently lower levels of oxygen. If the soil is well-drained, the particles themselves, in aggregates known as crumbs, will remain wet, but the water will, to a large extent, run away, leaving films of water around the particles. As it drains, clean, highly oxygenated air will take its place. The balance between sufficient water-retention to supply the needs of the developing seeds and the necessity for fairly frequent watering is what characterizes a good seed compost. It will not dry out quickly, but will allow for periodical changes of air by means of its free-draining qualities. Plant roots use up oxgygen and give off carbon dioxide, so this is not just a formula for success with seeds, but with all plants.

Light

Seeds in the resting state are not affected by changes in light intensity or duration, but some seeds become strongly light-sensitive once they have started to absorb water. Some, like primulas, require light for germination, and this quality is even more striking in foxgloves. What is noticeable about both is that they germinate well in woodland glades and not under trees and so important is this to the welfare of the seedlings that they can measure light quality.

It is not uncommon at all for plants to be sensitive to the duration and intensity of light—in fact it is an almost universal quality of plants, many of which fail to distinguish between length of light and intensity and react to the total quantity received in terms of candlepower. In some cases intense flashes of very bright light will produce the same effects as much longer periods at lower light levels.

Glade-loving plants, however, produce seeds which are capable of not only sensing the amount of light, but also its wavelength. A canopy of green leaves produces a light at the woodland floor that has a predominance of red, and this will be received as a no-go signal and germination will not take place.

While the presence of light is essential for some—from a minute or so of illumination for some lettuces to fifteen or sixteen hours for birches—others require that light be absent. *Gunnera manicata*, the enormous 'Giant Rhubarb' from the Brazilian jungles that grows by watersides in temperate gardens, requires pitch darkness for its germination. What you must not do is to peek to see if it has come up unless you do it in very dim conditions; flashes of bright light re-set the internal switch that inhibits germination and you have to start all over again.

Some alpines, including *Primula denticulata*, are sensitive to combinations of temperature and light, so that, although the temperature may not be high enough on its own, germination will occur if there is sufficient light. These factors break the dormancy of the seeds, or of the embryos within them, and it is dormancy which gives advanced seed-raisers the most problems.

Dormancy

Dormancy in seeds is a mechanism which stops them germinating in conditions or environments in which the young plants would stand a poor chance of developing to maturity and of producing in their turn crops of seed that would preserve the existence of the species.

Light sensitivity is an important factor, as was seen in the phenomenon of the Flanders poppies, more of whose seeds reached levels in the soil where they received sufficient light than ever before. There are, however, many other influences on the survivability of seedlings than light, and seeds have evolved to use them, either as triggers for germination or as cues for further slumber.

Perhaps the most shy, toe-in-the-water plant that we commonly grown in gardens is the tree-peony. If the seed lies about and gets dry after it has been shed, it will give up the ghost and die, convinced that there is no future. Given, on the other hand, the most ideal germinating conditions it will, even if it is sown straight from the pod, merely produce a long, questing, inquiring root in the first year. If all goes well and the root finds that the untrustworthy world has not produced a nasty surprise in the meantime, the shoot will develop in the following year. What is happening is that the seed is making absolutely certain, not only that the place and the time are right, but also that the environment shows signs of stability in the long term.

For this is what dormancy is all about—waiting for the safety that comes from the 'knowledge' that the environment will support life. Sometimes it is the armour of the seed—its coat—that provides the information. Rather like a passive version of Noah sending a dove over the waters to find dry land, *Campanula morettiana*, an exquisite high alpine from cliffs in the Dolomites of Italy, waits as an embryo safely within its seed-coat for at least two years. It *never* germinates in the first year but sits patiently until enough moisture has come into contact with it to wash out the inhibitory substances that its coat contains. It would be useless for it to be fooled by temporary moisture on what might subsequently turn out to be a barren ledge, so its dormancy mechanism allows it to be pretty sure that the place it is in will receive enough water to sustain it as an adult plant.

Among alpine gardeners a great many pots of seed of this campanula have been discarded as useless, as it may be three or even four years before it makes up its mind. Even more is this so with tree-peonies, whose half-germinated seeds must have been thrown away over the years by the ton. Check the tree-peony seed for germination by holding the big, black, hard seeds between finger and thumb and gently lifting. After a few weeks they should be firmly rooted and it only remains to wait for the next stage.

Of course, like all creation, plants and seeds can be fooled. Put the reluctant half-peonies in the refrigerator at about 5°C for ten days and then return them to the warmth and the logic of the process will tell them that surely another winter has passed in safety and that it is now spring again and time to go the whole hog.

Temperature is one of the main factors that plants use in providing their liferafts for their offspring. Many groups of plants would be much less successful than they are if this were not so. Alpines, for example, live in an environment where the growing season is much shorter than it is on the plains below, so newly-emerged plants need to be able to use as much of it as they can in order to have attained some size by the time the long winter sets in. It would not be much use if they germinated as soon as they were released and came into contact with warm soil—a few short weeks would see them killed by the oncoming cold. Temperature *per se* is not the governing factor; what triggers their germination is change of temperature and temperature gradient.

Alpine seeds will wait—they will lie dormant—until the temperature has fallen for a long period and then risen again. It may not fall far. Snow is an insulator, and the temperature range that matters is quite a high one, between 0° and 5°C. That this is the range in which the anomalous expansion of water takes place is not insignificant.

Some seeds, like many of the gentians, need several transitions through this range before they will germinate, while others need only one, but will go back to sleep if it is of too short a duration.

It is for these reasons that alpine gardeners like to sow their seeds either in the late autumn or in the very earliest days of the new year and then to leave them outside, where the frosts can get at them, and where the onset of the warmer weather of spring will act upon them in a natural way.

Many berries are best treated like this as well. The process is called vernalization; the 'convincing' a seed that spring has arrived and it is time to germinate. It is, of course, possible to trick seeds by using technology which, in terms of the length of time gardening has been going on, is very modern. The domestic refrigerator, set at just above freezing, provides just the right messages when alternated with the warmth of the kitchen. It may not do wonders for domestic harmony, but the seeds will react wonderfully.

With some plants, very high temperatures indeed are necessary for germination to be achieved. Some Australian plants and others from regions where bush fires occur, react to the passage of fire by having their seeds germinate in

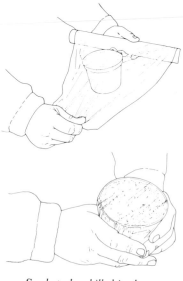

Seeds to be chilled in the refrigerator can be sown in their pots which are then wrapped in cling film wrap.

abundance after they themselves have been immolated. Curiously enough, the lower temperature of boiling water will also break the dormancy of most such seeds, especially those of the Legume family. Contrary to legend, on the other hand, it is quite unnecessary to apply fire to the seeds of *Eucalyptus* species; they germinate like cress on the surface of an ordinary compost with gentle bottom heat.

The seeds of the Monterey Pine, *Pinus radiata*, will germinate as soon as they are mature, but getting them intact out of their hard, bony cone is very difficult indeed. These cones are held on the tree unopened for up to forty years, so that they are eventually to be seen on very thick branches or even on the trunks. When they are very old they will open and release their seed, but before that it is only extreme heat that will induce them to open.

This is an adaptation to forest fire. The approaching heat opens the cones, whose seeds fall to the forest floor, which is relatively cool, as heat rises. After the fire has passed on and incinerated the selfless parents, the seed germinates enthusiastically under the influence of bottom heat from the warm soil and an abundance of nutrients from the ashes of the unfortunate dead.

Heat, like light, can re-set the 'trigger' for germination and induce a renewed period of dormancy. Some desert plants seem to be able to tell that the water that has fallen on their seed is only of the duration of a shower and is not going to continue. This is partly due to the fact that an insufficient proportion of the germination-inhibiting substances in their seed coats has been washed out, but it is also because the coolness caused by a decent amount of rain has not lasted long enough and the renewed heat has induced a further period of dormancy.

There are some seeds that not only have dormant embryos but also have impermeable seed-coats. There are two ways round the latter problem; one is to file, chip, or abrade the coat—the other is to sow outside in spring. What will happen then is that the weather and soil organisms will gradually destroy the seed coat, leaving the embryo exposed to the effects of temperature during the winter and the following spring, but now in the presence of water. Its dormancy will be broken and it should germinate the following spring. Several species of hawthorn demonstrate this combined resistance.

The problem with the tree-peony was that, while its root would grow in ordinary sowing conditions, it then required a cold spell, followed by warmth, in order that its nervousness about its new environment should be sufficiently overcome for it to put forth a shoot. A few plants are even more cagey than this, needing an initial cold period, then a warm one in which to develop a root, and then another cold-warm cycle to induce shoot production. This is termed double dormancy (as opposed to epicotyl dormancy in the peony) and it is of importance to those gardeners who would like to try *Smilacina racemosa* or lily-of-the-valley from seed.

To be dogmatic when talking about anything that is within the purview of Nature is idiotic, of course. Voices of readers of this will be heard loud in the land claiming germination of these dormant seeds with no trouble at all— no alternating periods of warmth and cold and no treatment beyond that which they give to their annuals.

They will no doubt be speaking the truth, but what do they mean by germination? What proportion of the seeds have come up? It is very likely that a very small proportion will emerge because Nature is not stupid and she makes allowances for the low chance that the species may be well served by those few individuals that have germinated idiosyncratically, while those bound by dormancy have found that events have passed them by.

In saying that *Campanula morettiana* always waits for two years, I am being dogmatic, I suppose, but not nearly as much as I was when, as a youngster, I argued with an eminent and much older plantsman who told me of the plant's requirements. I visited him with my seed-pan and arrogantly (or so it seems now) thrust it at him so that he might see the crop of seedlings sown the same year. He quietly took me to his frame and presented for my inspection a pan of the same size in which there were well over one hundred seedlings, beautifully spaced from a most expert sowing of two years previously. I retired, cheeks aflame, bearing sadly home my precious burden of little plants, of which there were just four.

I pricked them out with exquisite care and returned the pan to a frame. Nothing happened the following year, but the year after that I had an *embarras de richesse*, from the judicious giving-away of which I was able to salve some shreds of popularity among my alpine-gardening fellows.

Many plants—some of them ubiquitous weeds—have different sorts of seeds that germinate after varying periods of time, while others have seeds with varying degrees of inbuilt dormancy. The majestic giant echiums of the Canary Isles are best sown by the seed being scattered broadcast from a whole seed-head. They will germinate over a period of years, so that the gardener need not fear a really cold winter which might take the plant clean from his garden otherwise. Clovers, too, exhibit this phenomenon, although to the detriment, this time, of the gardener, who cannot understand why his lawn keeps on getting choked with clover even when he has spent a fortune in time and money in getting rid of it.

A number of plants have seeds that link the qualities of dormancy with the exigencies of seed-dispersal. Rather than rely upon a mechanism that recognizes that the time and place are right for germination, even though such a place may be quite close to the parent plants, these need to be 'told' that they have travelled a good distance away.

Such seeds employ animals as vehicles. There are many other seeds that do this as well, but they rely on seren-dipity—the mere hope that a sufficient number will have been taken on a journey to ensure adequate distribution. They may be adapted to hook on to the wool (or the woollen garments) of passing animals, or they may be dropped in mud of such a viscosity that it will adhere to the feet of land animals or birds. Mistletoes have sticky berries that become so firmly attached to the beaks of birds that their frantic swipes at a convenient branch are only suffi-cient to dislodge the berries if the stickiness adheres to what will become the host trees.

The true travellers, though, will travel within an animal, be it a land-based one or a bird. Among their number are the fruits that are good to eat. The provision of apples, pears, plums and peaches is not for our benefit at all; it is merely another example of Nature's drive to preserve the species—not to give us preserves. Animals that eat such fruits, or other ones that are attractive to them, ingest the seeds and expel them at a distance from the parent plants that may amount to many miles.

The acids in the digestive tracts of the animals leach substances from the seed coats that inhibit germination and allow the seed to 'know' that it has completed its journey. After that, it is subject to the same contingencies that govern germination generally.

These seeds will probably germinate in time if the place is right and they have not travelled. It will just take a lot longer, as micro-organisms and weather gradually break down the seed-coats. This is just as well for us, as there is an alternative, if we are patient, to soaking the seeds in strong solutions of acids. This is a practice that has been used by professional gardeners for a long time, but it is not to be recommended to the amateur, whose garden shed is a dangerous enough place already, nor to those without laboratory training, who might not know that there is a great difference in dramatic effect between adding water to an acid and adding an acid to water.

Luckily, boiling water, while not as efficient as acids, will do the job sufficiently well in the majority of cases to allow a decent proportion of the seeds to develop.

Viability

The viability of a seed is its potential length of life. It is a much-misunderstood aspect of seedsmanship, but the matter is easily put right.

Seeds, like all living things, have life-spans, but they are not regular, or predictable within a narrow range, as are those of animals and of quite a lot of plants. They depend to a very large extent on the conditions in which they have to spend their lives.

Perfect germination conditions might be thought of as ending the life of a seed, but this is a misleading notion, as life itself does not cease; it merely changes its condition. True death of a seed occurs when its contents die and lose the ability to be transformed into a new plant.

Before what are really very modern times, it was very difficult for the plant-collectors to ensure that the seed they sent home arrived in a living condition. For many species it did not matter too much, as they were able to live for a long time, but for some, such as a great many Asiatic Primulas, delay was fatal, as their lifespans as seeds are very short.

A collector, high in the Himalaya or the mountains of Burma and Western China, would send his seeds by runner to the nearest port. That this alone could take two or three weeks would be enough to see some seeds off, although only a very few. He was then reliant on having an efficient agent who could be depended upon to obtain rapid posting of the seeds upon a ship bound for the right home port and, further, upon rapid distribution and sowing at the other end. Should a sailing ship, making for England via Good Hope, become becalmed in the Doldrums, hope would fade with every day that passed. Rounding the Horn for the gardens of America suggested even worse fates.

Even the advent of the steamship and the canals of Panama and Suez did little to help. It was the aircraft and the introduction of refrigeration that finally allowed collectors to beat the deadline deeply built-in to the 'consciousness' of the seeds. For it is temperature, in this case coldness, and water-content that are the factors that can prolong the lifespans of seeds (or, by their mismanagement, curtail them) and it is these that we shall see as the main considerations in the storage of seeds at home.

Harvesting and the Storage of Seed

Collecting Seed

Professional gardeners of the old school were, by and large, uncomplicated men. Those of them that I have had on my staff, like their younger colleagues, tended to have scant respect for the more neurotic aspects of their boss's character, but were more inclined to be blunt than to tease, as the youngsters do.

One year, I was fretting about a monstrous crop of seed that was developing on a species of magnolia. I wanted to maximize my collection of this seed, as it was not set very often and I had requests from quite a few seed houses to supply it in large quantities. The trouble was that the seed was 60ft (20m) up in the tree and there was thick vegetation below, as well as extremely well-trodden paths.

I suppose I had driven the poor chaps mad by going on about the problem. One of their number, possessed of an engaging stutter which advancing years had not ameliorated, eventually emerged from a prolonged silence.

'Why don't you c–c–cut the b ... y t-tree down?' he complained.

Harvesting seed is by no means easy. It is extremely time-consuming, occasionally dangerous, and always frustrating. Timing is of the essence, as seed must, in almost all cases, be gathered as it ripens, and it is at just that very point that you are very likely to find that it has beaten you to it and vanished.

If there were just one short period of the year when all the seeds became ready, life would be much simpler. As it is, there is hardly any time of the year when the seed-collector can allow his vigilance to relax, and regular patrols around the garden are vital if everything is to be garnered that is required for sowing.

Dispersal Mechanisms

A seed in its green state is no good at all. It has not properly differentiated into the tissues that will form the embryo, and its water content is far too high. As it ripens, its water content drops rapidly, as does that of the structures surrounding the seed. Once the seed is completely formed, it is not necessary for further water and nutrients to reach it, and it will become cut off from the rest of the plant by a link of desiccated tissue, so that it can become firm and dry. Its colour will change at this stage, usually from some shade of green to a neutral colour such as brown or black.

The surrounding tissues—most often the calyx of the

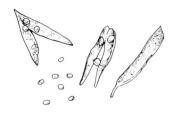

The rare and tender Adenocarpus foliosus *can often only be maintained by means of its explosively dispersed seed.*

flower, or the walls of what was the ovary and became the seed pod—become very dry and, as extreme dryness occurs, can suddenly, and with great violence, perform prodigious feats of gunnery.

A weed, now found in temperate gardens all over the world, whence it has been transported with the international exchanges of plants (the ultimate example of using animals for dispersal?) and called 'Penny Cress' or 'Poppers', displays its predilection for artillery practice at the slightest touch. Weeding among your garden plants, you will be bent down in the ideal posture for the mischievous thing to fire a hearty salvo straight into your eyes.

That the human eye is adapted to react with extraordinary rapidity of reflex to objects, no matter how small, that approach it, is no defence. The minute, round seeds fly at such a rate that the blink fails to thwart them. One lesson to be learned is that you should always wear spectacles when weeding; the other is that the explosive power of some seed-dispersal mechanisms should never be underestimated.

The ballistic expertise of the capsule is demonstrated perfectly by many species of *Viola*. As ripeness occurs, the seed-vessel splits into five, and each fifth, as it further dries and turns from green to a light tan hue, clasps its quota of seeds in an increasingly iron grip. As the process continues, the segments come to lie further and further apart from each other, until the whole looks like a pale brown star. From now on the piece is loaded and it will require only a smidgeon of sunlight or a faint touch for each fifth to go off. Fire one! Right in the eyes again.

A champion shooter among plants that will grow where frosts are relatively light is *Euphorbia mellifera*. It comes from the Canary Isles and makes quite a large shrub, with apple-green foliage and honey-scented, maroon-tan flowers. Its seed capsules are just like grape-shot and about as hard, and it is almost an impossibility to extract the seed from them before they are absolutely *à point*.

There is no deliberate cocking of the firing mechanism with this plant. One moment the pod is as rock-hard as ever; the next it has split with a loud report and the seeds are twenty feet away. The ensuing problem is not just that it is very difficult indeed to find the seeds—every finch in the neighbourhood will race to beat the others (and you) to get at them.

The way to obtain a harvest of these seeds is to be very vigilant indeed on a hot, sunny day in late summer. At the first sound of gunfire, every branched cluster of a dozen or more seed pods should be cut off with a piece of stem and thrust, head downward, into one of the large, stout paper sacks that animal feeds come in.

The result is great fun. Like that conjuring trick in which the magician causes a paper bag to jerk as if an egg had just landed in it, your paper sack will twitch and crack as the internal bombardment rises to a climax. A day or two later, after the stragglers have performed, you will have a final haul of seed, neatly trapped and perfectly ripe. It is, too, one of the most eager germinators of all seed, emerging just a few days after sowing in the early spring.

Explosive seed *must* be contained, or it is lost for ever. Paper bags are the answer in almost all cases, although large ones are not always necessary. With some plants, individual, small bags can be tied round the drying seed-heads, allowing gas exchange to go on and heat to play its part. This also encourages ripening, as dews and rain are kept off. When the seed has fallen into the bag, the stem can be cut, the bag returned to the open-end-up position, and the harvest can be carried off for storage.

The same idea can be used for wind-borne seeds. Nothing is more totally frustrating than to see precious seed being blown away into oblivion and nothing is more funny than watching a frantic gardener racing about trying to catch a few of the precious parachutes before they stream away far beyond his reach. It takes a certain strength of wind to detach such seeds—they react to the agitation it causes and, of course, to the extra degree of drying that a wind causes. Such a wind is likely to be faster than a man can run, so to be unprepared is folly.

It is worth noting, however, that with some types of wind-dispersed seed, a few will be left behind when the majority have taken off. This is true, too, of quite a few plants that disperse their seed by the drying-up of the capsule. The Horned Poppies (*Glaucium* spp.) have very long, slender pods that split longitudinally from the top. The combination of the splitting and the shivering that wind causes, disperses the seeds at the ends of the pods first, while those at the bases persist, often for several days. All hope is not gone, then, when the tardy gardener finds a mass of split, straw-like pods; he may still obtain a worthwhile amount of seed from Nature's way of taking out an insurance policy against putting all her eggs in one basket.

True poppies (*Papaver* spp.) have large pods that develop holes right round their tops, out of which the seed is shaken like pepper. *Meconopsis*, which includes the Himalayan blue poppies, is similar, but its pods are elongatedly oval. After quite a period of dispersal, there will still be some seed left in these cases, but keen vigilance and a paper bag will ensure a rich haul.

The paper bag treatment is a good one for seed that is very fine. *Hydrangea sargentiana* is a tall plant with 8ft

A single seedhead of
Hydrangea sargentiana *will*
provide more than enough seed
if it is shaken into a large
paper or plastic bag.

(2.5m) stems, large, velvety leaves, and very large flat flower heads. These heads are of the 'lacecap' type, in which the flower-appeal comes from the large, sterile florets that surround a mass of tiny, fertile ones.

It is pretty futile to try to extract the seed from these, as each one is about the size of a sweet-pea seed itself, and contains several seeds, each of which is no bigger than a grain of ground pepper. In mid-autumn, when the last vestige of colour has gone from the flowers, the flower heads can be cut off and shaken vigorously into a large bag. A dozen heads will provide enough seed to produce an acre of plants, so sowing has to be circumspect, even though you have only enough seed to fill a teaspoon. Sow a pinch and give the rest away.

Rhododendrons use the dispersal of their seed as a sort of sideways form of dormancy. Dispersal can occur any time from late autumn to mid-winter, depending on what species is in question. The seedlings of rhododendrons are extremely tiny at first and they would not stand up to severe winters, nor to having falling leaves suffocate them in autumn. They are, therefore, programmed to be dropped to their germination-place at the optimum time for them to begin developing in the spring. The largest-leaved ones tend to be the last to release their seed, but with them all, some seed is left in the tenacious capsule for periods of some months.

This applies, too, to other members of the Ericaceae, such as *Enkianthus*, and they serve to show that the harvesting season is a much longer one than people usually think. As soon as one or two of a cluster of pods begins to split, the whole should be cut off and put in a paper bag and taken to a warm shed, where ripening can continue. You will then be sure of having dry seed well away from the wet winter.

Cyclamen display one of the more bizarre phenomena of timing, both of seed-dispersal and of germination. It is possible to have cyclamen of various species in flower in the garden for much of the year, and the appearance of their leaves occurs in due and varying seasons, too. Thus *C. hederifolium* produces its leaves in autumn, while *C. orbiculatum* does so in early winter. What is extraordinary is that their seeds germinate at the same time as the leaves appear on the adult plants, although there is a logic to it that is irresistible.

Even more strange is that, although species may flower in mid-winter or mid-summer, or anywhere in between, the seeds of all the species ripen and are dispersed in late summer. It is thus a good thing for the would-be collector of cyclamen seed to know this, otherwise he will never think of visiting all his species at the same time.

Cyclamen seeds are coated with a sugary, sticky substance that ants find totally delicious. They will struggle manfully for hours to get the seeds down into their nests, and that is the last you will ever see of them unless you have been strictly on the *qui vive*. The stems bearing the ball-like capsules coil tightly, tucking the pods close to the parent plants. When dispersal is imminent, the stem uncoils, and the capsule rolls away from the parent. It then splits progressively from a point opposite to that where the stem (peduncle) is attached to the pod.

With *C. persicum*, the peduncle never coils up, so extra vigilance has to be employed, but with it, as with all cyclamen, the seed should be gathered as the pods start to split, and it should be sown immediately. Germination will occur when the leaves appear on the adults if it is sown fresh, but if the seed is allowed to become dry, it may come up only sparsely and after a year or so, it may never perform at all.

The ardent seed-raiser's potting shed, his kitchen, or even his sitting room may become festooned with paper containers of varying kinds in which are stems with seed pods attached which are drying off. Another method, useful with such things as alstroemerias, whose dispersal is by explosion, is to put the pods in a seed tray after they have been gathered as they turn brown. They can be covered with a sheet of paper so as to contain the seeds, but this can be a slightly unsure method unless the paper is firmly secured. A blast of wind through an opening door can undo a great deal of patient work, especially if it is not noticed for a while.

It is highly advisable to collect large seed pods at an early stage so that water does not lodge among the seeds and set up deterioration. Irises, for instance, should have the pods removed as soon as the slightest split occurs. Taken indoors, they will finish drying very quickly and will not escape by being flung about. Watch out for earwigs and other nasties, though. They seem to spot a split seed-pod in a flash as a potential home and you will not be very popular if they end up in the furniture or adding an exotic flavour to the soup.

Tree seeds

The magnolia that posed such a problem to me dropped its bright orange seeds to the ground, and I had no alternative to making early-morning collecting expeditions to pick up the seeds from the paths before they were crushed by passing feet. Those not on the paths had to be rooted about for among the surrounding vegetation. When seed is required from tall trees, there is little one can do apart from waiting for it to drop. Foresters may ascend into the tree canopy to make their collection, but the average gardener is not an expert tree-climber and must make do with what he can get from below.

Some tree seeds are easy to spot, like the brightly-coloured magnolia seeds, while others are big enough, like acorns and horse-chestnuts, to be found without difficulty. Many, though, have dispersal systems that take their smaller seeds away and it is with these that the gardener must exercise his most acute watchfulness. Winged seeds, like those of acers, can be obtained by frequent visits to the neighbourhood of the tree, where one must search about for what one can find. The chances of mixing seeds from different species is high, though, and in the final analysis a ladder may be the answer to the problem.

Luckily, one does not usually want to gather large quantities of seed from trees. Just a few will usually do, and it is not an exercise that the gardener has to enjoy very often. Where problems do often occur is when a promise is given, usually at a convivial function at which the thirst engendered by a hard day's gardening is being assuaged, to provide some seed of a tree for a neighbour. The solution is quite simple: never make such promises.

Worthwhile seeds

Every gardener who has gone in for seed-sowing on any sort of scale will have come across species that simply never germinate. This seems to negate the idea that seeds want to turn into plants, and it would, were it not that whenever this happens there is something wrong.

This may often be some cultural factor—a matter of poor compost, intermittent drying and wetting—in fact, it could be one of a great many things. Occasionally, however, failure is caused because the seed is no good in the first place.

This is not to mention those occasions when a seed house has supplied bad seed, stored perhaps for too many years in the hope of maximizing profits, but to point out a natural failure in seed formation.

It is quite possible for a great deal of time and effort to be taken in harvesting seeds of certain plants, only to find that the exercise was a complete waste of time. At first glance, the seeds may appear to be first-class; plump, and of a good colour, but under really close examination they will be found to be lacking embryos. This is called 'unfilled' seed, and it can even be sent out in good faith by very good seed houses. How much more is it likely to be sown after collection in the garden of an amateur?

For years I received seeds of *Telopaea truncata*, the Tasmanian 'Waratah', from a seed company for whom I had and have the highest regard. Never once did a single seedling appear, and yet a batch sent to me by a lady in Tasmania came up like cress. The seedsman and I discussed the failure and agreed that his source was supplying unfilled seed, and the lesson we both learned was that one should always take a sample and open up the seeds to see what is inside.

Most species of *Olearia* fail to set true seed in cultivation. Why this should be I am not sure, although climate must have something to do with it. Seed of *O. macrodonta*, for example, is set in great profusion but, except in an unusual year when about one half of one per cent of seeds will be filled, they are all dud.

Another genus which, like *Olearia*, comes from New Zealand and has flowers like daisies, is *Celmisia*. There are many species, mostly what I perversely and inaccurately call evergreen herbaceous plants, and they are nearly all very difficult indeed to germinate. I tried them for years, particularly one (*C. coriacea*), whose intensely silver, sword-shaped leaves and large, white daisies on tall stems particularly appealed to me. Not one seedling ever appeared, no matter whether I obtained seed from seedsmen in Britain, from New Zealand, or from my own few plants.

Eventually, however, a New Zealand friend trekked down from the North Island to the very tip of the South, where he took himself to Secretary Island on the coast of the Southland National Park. He very kindly sent a generous batch of seed that he collected there from the recalcitrant species, and it germinated with an incredible abandon. That was not the end of the story; the next generation of plants, grown from that seed, set in its turn seed with just as much *joie de vivre* as the parents.

It is a stern lesson that all good gardeners have to learn that dogmatism has no place in the make-up of those who would be successful in dealing with nature. No species should ever be written off as ungrowable from seed. One day, somehow, you will obtain good seed of what has always seemed an impossible plant. When you do, treasure the source, be it a place or a person and if you are such a source yourself, be generous in the time you spend in harvesting and in the trouble you take in giving your precious seed away to as many people as possible.

Seed storage

Cleaning seed

It is a great mistake to try to store seed that is mixed up with bits of seed-pod, leaves, or insects. The vegetable component will tend to rot and infect the seed, while the animal fraction might well eat it.

It is also well-nigh impossible to obtain an even sowing with bits and pieces in among the seed and, furthermore, as soon as the sowing is watered, all kinds of moulds will fasten on the dead material and soon spread to the seed.

Cleaning, then, is vital. Inexperienced handlers of seed, particularly those who have ample means but a paucity of worthwhile activities with which to occupy their time, will tend to acquire a collection of sieves with a great variety of mesh-sizes in the fond hope that they can winnow any size of seed neatly enough to leave the detritus behind.

In my salad days, I attempted this just once. I tried to sieve seed of a *Draba* species (an alpine cushion plant with yellow flowers) and used the family flour sieve. After much activity the seeds were permanently and inextricably enmeshed, the sieve was trampled flat by an enraged foot and cast clangingly into the dustbin, and nobody spoke to me for a week. Elaboration is the vice of the tyro.

Some folk winnow their seed in their hand, by blowing the lighter gubbins away and hoping to leave the denser seed snug in their palm. The dangers are many. One cough or, even more surely, a sneeze, will in one fell swoop achieve in terms of dispersal what nature has been aiming at for millennia. Should some repulsive, crawly bug suddenly drop from the pod into the waiting hand, the resulting reflex jerk will have much the same distributory effect. Murphy's law applies to this practice as to almost no other.

While larger seeds can be gathered very easily without extraneous material becoming mixed up with it, smaller ones are almost always adulterated with odds and ends. It is sensible to ignore this until the crop has been brought indoors into a draught-free place, when the whole lot should be put on to a sheet of paper that is quite large. Mostly, the biggest size of typing paper will do.

Using the palm sides of the straightened fingers, a light pass over the pile of seed will flatten it out, leaving husks and bits at the periphery, from which they can be swept away with the fingertips. To repeat this several times will sort out all but the smallest bits, which can then be removed by agitation.

If a crease is made in the paper, gentle shaking to and fro along the line of the crease will separate the seed from the remaining rubbish, which can then be swept away with the fingertip, leaving the seed concentrated in a chute, down which it can be slid, to come to rest in its storage vessel.

It is a mistake to procrastinate about seed-cleaning, and it is an excellent discipline to attend to the job for each batch as it is harvested, otherwise the whole business becomes an excruciating bore, patience is lost, and the job gets done in a slipshod manner.

Berries and fruits are dealt with by different people in different ways. I prefer to dry berries off as soon as possible

Extracting seeds of Rosa
rubrifolia *from the hips before
an autumn sowing.*

and, when the process is complete, to extract the seed from
all the berries I can. Many gardeners complain about non-
germination of the minute Mountain Ash, *Sorbus reducta*.
The fact is that they sow the berries whole. If they took the
seed from the berries and sowed them, they would find this
tiny tree most generous and it would be seen in alpine
gardens far more than it is. This, too is a job that is better
done in the lazy days of autumn than in the sowing days of
early spring, when everything is happening at once.

Some fruits have their seeds embedded in a fleshy mess,
and it is often very difficult to dry them off before moulds
take over and ruin everything. One example is the rare and
rather tender *Cornus capitata*, an Asian version of the
American dogwoods. Its fruits are like giant raspberries,
and they start to rot almost as soon as they are picked. They
have, too, to be picked as soon as they turn from being
creamy-yellow to being flushed with red, otherwise every
bird within the district will home in for a free feast. The
hard seeds are quite easily, if messily, extracted from the
flesh, and they can then be laid out to dry and stored with
no further trouble.

Labelling

From the moment a batch of seed is harvested, it should be
labelled accurately. This applies most particularly to those
seeds that ripen in succession, as there is nothing more
frustrating than to find that you have two or three piles of
seed which you suspect are from the same species, but about
which you cannot be sure. *Every* batch of seed should carry
its own label.

It is difficult to have patience with those who think it a
sign of expertise to have no labels in their gardens. It is, in
fact, an indication of ignorance of the most base sort acting
in concert with conceit of a high degree. The most knowledgeable gardeners are those who are terrified of forgetting
names because there are so many with which they are
familiar and yet so very many more still to learn. Middle-
aged, truly expert plantsmen often forget names and tend to
blame their age. It is usually not so; they have seen the huge
body of knowledge that can never be assimilated in a
lifetime and it has daunted them. They defend themselves
wisely by resorting to meticulous and comprehensive labelling systems, never more so than when dealing with seeds,
whose characteristics are not as engraveable upon the
memory as are those of plants.

The paper bag, or whatever is the receptacle of first
receipt, should be labelled with the full name of the plant
and the date of harvesting. It is superficially terribly clever
to write 'japonica' or 'nuttallii', and it is a favourite trick of

half-grown planty people to use such isolated epithets in conversation. One such a character discoursed for fully five minutes about *Rhododendron nuttallii* to me one day, and his exclusive use of the specific epithet without the generic name led me to reply in terms of *Cornus nuttallii*. That I must have appeared just as stupid as he did not alter the fact that I do not get my seeds in the mess that he would if he used the same slackness in his labelling as in his talk.

Every subsequent packet or vessel into which the seed is put should be as carefully labelled and, most importantly, the label for the seed tray should be made *before the seed is removed from its packet and sown.*

Temperature and Moisture

There is a planthunter, an astute and extraordinarily brave man, no stranger to attacks by bandits and to extreme privation brought upon by heat, altitude, and lack of supplies, who spent not so long ago a whole year in a remote part of the Middle East. On this occasion he took his wife with him, and it was she who normally received his airmailed batches of seed, cleaned, and stored them.

Because they were both abroad, a friend, a lady of some good plant knowledge and of great conscientiousness, undertook to carry out the wife's role, which she did with great care, labelling and packeting for many hours at a time.

When, however, those to whom the seed was distributed came to expect results from their sowings, there were virtually none and the poor man's year turned out to have been wasted. The good lady had been so concerned for the welfare of the seed that she had stored it all in her sitting room, where there was a constant temperature of 21°C, night and day.

Heat substantially reduces the life of seeds, and in the presence of moisture it can rapidly kill them. On the other hand, cold can greatly increase their longevity, even beyond that which is theirs in nature.

Moisture is anathema to the resting seed. It is as damaging as deprivation of sleep is to an animal which, disturbed at regular intervals over a long period, becomes disoriented and eventually dies.

Seed should be stored in a cool, dry place, where there is a gentle circulation of air and where moulds and miasmas do not lurk. It does not matter if freezing temperatures occur occasionally, and something around 5–10°C is ideal. A clean garden shed, or a porch which does not receive frequent blasts of centrally-heated air, are good places. Living rooms or kitchens are not.

Containers

Apart from those fleshy seeds, like magnolias, that must be sown immediately and not dried at all, most seeds should be thoroughly dry before being stored. If they are not, it will not matter in the least what sorts of storage containers are used; the seed will inevitably rot.

Tobacco tins and coffee jars are often advocated as receptacles for stored seed, but I have found that there is nothing to beat the kinds of envelopes that are used when wages are paid in cash. They are not sealed by licking a gum, but have a self-sealing compound on them that can be used twice or three times — that is to say, the envelopes can be opened for the occasional inspection and then resealed.

Anyone who goes in for saving seed on more than a very small scale would be well advised to invest in a cabinet. This can be just a rough cupboard, made up at home and installed in the potting shed. With plenty of shelves and, preferably, pigeonholes, a large number of envelopes can be stored in some degree of order. This system — envelopes in a cabinet — has preserved seed in storage for me better than anything else. Because other methods are suggested by gardeners of equal or greater experience than myself, I can only recommend what I have personally found to work best, although I think that the air circulation afforded by the above method is to the advantage of the seeds.

When it comes to sending seed to friends, or to seed companies, it is amazing how many people fail to appreciate the way in which seeds will escape, Houdini-like, from the most tightly sealed wrapping. One has so often received parcels in the mail, in which are assortments of envelopes, twists of paper, and odd packets, out of which the seeds have spilled and become inextricably mixed so that the whole consignment has been rendered useless.

This can be very tiresome indeed, especially when one knows that the sender has gone to great trouble to obtain the seed. One is faced with writing a letter of thanks in which, if one is not to cause hurt to the feelings of the sender, one must tell lies. This is not too difficult if the seeds have been sent from far away. Someone nearer at hand may well turn up and want to see the fine crop of seedlings that you have raised from the seed that you threw away.

To transport seed by letter there is nothing better than the little, semi-transparent envelopes that are sold by dealers in postage stamps. They are so precisely made and they seal so perfectly that the smallest seeds will not make their way out of them. It is, after all, quite unnecessary to send people huge quantities of small seeds — just a pinch will do. Large crops can be sent to seed houses in the wages envelopes, preferably reinforced with 1in (2.5cm) wide cellophane tape.

Records

While labelling is absolutely vital, the keeping of records is merely wise. The absence of records leads to embarrassment and to the sort of wistful regret that comes to people who find that they know a lot more now than they did when the records might have been made.

If you are sent seed of some highly desirable plant and it eventually grows into a garden specimen, it is a very good idea indeed to have on record the source of the seed. I shall never forget the crushing feelings of remorse that I felt after having loftily offered seed of a rare plant to a friend who accepted it kindly, forbearing to mention that he had, at great inconvenience to himself, obtained the original for me in the first place.

Labels themselves can carry condensed information as to the source of seed and the date of sowing, but it is far better for a card index system to be set up, the very writing of which will impress the facts upon the memory, besides its acting as an instant source of relief from mortification. Further, should disaster strike and the plants be lost, it is pretty sensible to be able to know where to turn for a possible replenishment in the form of new seed.

When it becomes a capital sin not to keep records is if you have been in receipt of seeds that carry collectors' numbers.

Professional plant collectors, who may be acknowledged plant-hunters, either acting alone or as members of expeditions, number their batches of seed so that a number refers to a particular plant in the wild. They will usually have sent pressed material to a botanical institution, where it will be kept with its number in the herbarium.

Should you make the acquaintance of such people, either as friends, or by contributing towards a share of their collectings in the wild, you will find yourself receiving batches of seed which will bear a name and a number, or sometimes (and here it becomes most exciting) a number on its own. This number *must* accompany *all* the seedlings that arise from the seed, but must *not* be used with seed of the second generation, when it will be likely to have become adulterated by cross-breeding in the garden.

Collectors' numbers put us in touch with the true wild species, many of which may no longer exist in our gardens because of the infusion of other blood. This is particularly true of such genera as *Rhododendron*, whose morals are loose, to say the least. Furthermore, specimens within a species can vary quite a lot, and by growing plants from different numbers within the same species, we can learn a great deal about them and can report back our findings to the collectors, to whom this information can be of the greatest interest. These variations may be of flower colour, of form, of garden-worthiness, or of hardiness. Unless we know which number we are talking about, the information is useless, and unless we keep records, we shall lose the numbers.

Collectors' numbers almost always have two components. Firstly, there will be one or more letters, and secondly, one or more figures. The letters usually stand for the collector's name, or for the name of a group. L. & S., for instance, stands for Ludlow and Sherriff, collectors in the Far East in the mid-twentieth century. SBEC represents the Sino-British Expedition to China of 1981, while L. is assigned to Roy Lancaster, who has made many solo collecting trips in that country. L/S, on the other hand, tells that seed collected by staff of the Shanghai Botanic Garden was sent to Mr. Lancaster, who then in turn redistributed the seed.

Thus, *Rhododendron* aff. *tatsienense* L.951 means: a species of *Rhododendron*, very much like *R.tatsienense*, but not yet positively identified as such or as possibly a new species, collected by Roy Lancaster and given his number 951 in the wild.

The batch of some fifty specimens which I raised from this seed is described on my card-index records, and every one of the plants carries a label with that number when it is planted out, sold, or given away, or otherwise leaves the company of its fellows which are lined up behind one main label.

Lest it should be thought that all this is a bit abstruse and quite beyond the experience of most amateur gardeners, it is worth pointing out that just about all gardeners, no matter how humble they may think themselves, will find themselves sowing wild-collected seed bearing a collectors' number once they become truly involved with first division gardening, which is what growing from seed certainly is.

What Seeds to Sow

There are some seeds which there is no point in sowing at all. Unfilled seeds are, of course, useless, and the experienced grower will soon spot seed that is not good, whether it be from lack of contents or for any other reason.

There is a great temptation, as one becomes more and more fascinated with the subject, for one to spend a lot of energy, space, and facilities in sowing seeds that are a complete waste of time. It is, for instance, silly to sow the Hungarian Oak, *Quercus frainetto*, unless one has a very large garden. No matter how beguiling its very large leaves and stately habit may appear, just one tree will eventually occupy the whole of a small garden and block out the light to the windows of the house.

It is, too, rather unthinking to sow more than just a very few seeds of *Paulownia tomentosa*. This very fast-growing tree can either be grown as a flowering specimen, in which case its blue-mauve, foxglove-like flowers are supremely decorative at the ends of the naked branches in the early spring, or several can be 'stooled' each year and fed hard to produce tropical-looking, very large, velvety foliage. A packet of seed will be enough to cover the surface of two seed trays and will produce enough plants to fill about three acres of land. Obviously, one 3in (8cm) pot with about a dozen seeds will suffice, given that it is a species that germinates very readily.

More important, though, because it is not governed merely by common sense, but by the laws of genetics, and is therefore not so obvious, is the danger of time-wasting caused by sowing seeds of cultivars. These are often offered in seed catalogues, and it does not appear at first glance that there is anything wrong with sowing them.

Indeed, *prima facie* there is not. You will get some sort of a result, but it is likely to be very disappointing and not at all what you expected.

Plants are classified into genera, which are in turn subdivided into species—for example, *Camellia japonica*. The genus is *Camellia*, and the species is *C.japonica*. This species has quite large, glossy leaves and small, light red flowers with nine petals. If you sow seed of the species you will consistently get plants like the parents, although there will be some slight variation, for which, if you were very patient (and in this case, completely crazy), you might selectively breed.

The Japanese, though, did so much work on the species so many centuries ago that, when the Honourable East India Company brought plants to Europe in the eighteenth century, there were varieties with large, fully double flowers, and the colours were in many shades of pink as well as red, and included white. These varieties can only be kept constant by cloning; that is to say that they have to be vegetatively propagated by cuttings or by grafting. To try to propagate them from seed produces plants which are totally different from their parents.

What is more, the overwhelming majority of the seedlings will be of far less worth than the parents. In fact, some of them will be likely to emerge as little different from the small-flowered, original species. It would take the production of thousands of seedlings to make at all likely the arrival of a plant that was sufficiently good to warrant a place in the garden.

It is, of course, a different matter if you have decided to go in for plant breeding. You will then sow seeds from cultivars (which is what garden varieties are called) but you will do it on a large scale and with a considerable amount of forethought and planning. This is a highly legitimate occupation for gardeners, as we shall see later, but the point is that, for those who wish to get the best results from what might be termed a 'normal' amount of seed-sowing, cultivars are best ruled out.

Sometimes it is a very poor idea indeed to sow cultivar seedlings, although for a different reason. Take, for example, a plant called *Viola* 'Irish Molly'. This delightful denizen of cottage gardens has a pansy flower in shades of green and chocolatey-brown. The great plantswoman Margery Fish described it has having a 'dirty brownish face', which does little justice to a truly captivating plant.

A few years ago it became almost unobtainable because, although it set little seed, gardeners insisted on sowing it and calling the results 'Irish Molly'. Furthermore, other pansies nearby that readily produced seed, would tend to cross-breed with it and deliver seedlings that were similar to, but not identical with the cultivar. The result was that these spurious seedlings were widely circulated, to the great detriment of Molly herself, who almost disappeared into total obscurity.

The dilution of good cultivars would never happen if all gardeners were scrupulous and completely understood the difference between a species and a cultivar. You just can not take seed from a cultivar and call the seedlings by the cultivar name. It is perfectly legitimate to call them, for example, Irish Molly Seedlings, but it is a truly heinous crime to bestow upon them the name of the cultivar itself.

There are, as with all rules, exceptions to the one governing the sowing of cultivar seeds. Perhaps it is best not to formulate the rule at all, so that sufficient experience can be allowed to be gained in the interest of finding out what the exceptions are. However, they are few, so the rule holds after all.

Deciduous azaleas, plants that can attain heights of well over 6ft (2m) and which make large, dense bushes in time, have flowers in the most spectacular colours and combinations of tones. Flaming reds, brilliant oranges and startling yellows occur, as well as delicate pinks and quiet golds. The cultivars, of which there are many, are difficult to propagate, and are best left to professionals, who can supply the artificial light, the heat, and the considerable skill that is necessary.

What is so different about them is that their seed hardly ever produces a plant that is not completely garden-worthy, and it is quite a commonplace occurrence for seedlings to turn out to be so similar to cultivated varieties as to be quite indistinguishable from them. A seedling of mine so resembles the cultivar 'Satan', with a dramatically beelzebubian shade of wicked red, that I cannot tell the two apart— although I have them properly labelled, I am glad to say. It would be wrong of me to label the seedling 'Satan'; I have it as 'Red Seedling'.

Perhaps the reason for this phenomenon is that the species of deciduous azalea that have been used in raising the cultivars all have very good garden flowers. One of them, properly called *Rhododendron luteum* (for while all rhododendrons are not azaleas, all azaleas are rhododendrons) and sometimes *Azalea pontica*, has flowers of the clearest light yellow and the most glorious scent. Seed from this will always give you beautiful results and a great many of the seedlings will turn out to be as close to the parents as makes no difference.

Hybrids obey the same rules as cultivars. Seed catalogues will often offer such things as *Aquilegia* Hybrids. These can give very good results if the strain is good and it is offered by a respectable seed house, but do not expect anything but a mixture to result. Seed of a hybrid will not produce plants like the parent; this is known as 'not coming true'. As most hybrids that gain garden space do so because they are better than either of their parents, there is not much point in sowing their seed, as you will be highly unlikely to gain by it.

A hybrid is denoted by an x between the generic name and another (hybrid) name that follows it. An example is *Camellia* x *williamsii*. Seed of this will not be at all like the parent, whereas seed of the species *C. saluenensis*, which is one of its parents with *C. japonica*, would be. The term in fact covers all crosses of the two species, many of which have cultivar names in their turn, like the famous 'Donation'. In general, it is better to stick for the most part to sowing species. The results will be reliable, and those specimens that do not come up to standard will serve to educate the gardener's eye so that, when he eventually becomes a bit adventurous and tries breeding, he will have had a little training in spotting good and bad plants.

To sow species is by no means to restrict oneself. The range that can be grown in gardens is truly enormous, and it must be confessed that species plants very often have flowers that are much more appealing to those with educated tastes than are the often blousy and overdone flowers of many cultivars. This applies very much in *Rhododendron*, most of whose species have flowers of great elegance and tranquil beauty, as opposed to the over-the-top flowers of the so-called Hardy Hybrids, which are the ones most usually found in garden centres.

Catalogues

It goes without saying that the best and most satisfying seed to sow is that which has been given to one by knowledgable friends (but not by those who merely think they know) or that which has arrived from some scientific or plant-hunting expedition. Most of us, though, will get the bulk of our seed from commercial sources, and it is as well to ensure that they are good ones.

The great seed houses are great because they provide very good seed. They mostly list items which are likely to be in large demand, though, and this means that if you are a grower of vegetables, annuals, or biennials, you will be very well catered for indeed.

When it comes to the more unusual things, and to such plants as the majority of trees and shrubs, it is necessary to turn to the catalogues of another sort of merchant. These do not usually go in for highly illustrated brochures, but often have extremely full and detailed lists of many hundreds of items. They are supremely tempting and may be found on the bedside tables of many gardeners during the winter months.

The journals of the horticultural societies of the world are where their addresses are to be found and most of them will ship seed to other countries, as there is no customs limitation on the transport of seed. Indeed, if you wish to send seed yourself to friends in other countries, the customs slip needs merely to be inscribed 'Flower seeds, no commercial value', and you will be sure that there will be no interference with them.

However, even these folks have to make a living, and while it is highly unlikely that they will ever offer anything in bad faith, they will expect you to know about things that do not 'come true', and they cannot be expected to annotate every item accordingly. The best of them publish notes in their catalogues which clarify such matters, as well as giving useful hints on sowing, so it is as well to spend a little time reading their introductions. Experience may ultimately lead you to disagree with them, but that is part of the fun.

Gardeners, like people everywhere who have specific interests, tend to form themselves into societies. These are either general or specialist in their appeal, and most gardeners who become society members find that they tend to join one of each. Generalist societies range from the great national horticultural ones to those that have a more local base, or have a particular bias, such as conservation. Specialist ones may deal with a wide grouping of plants, such as the Hardy Plant Society, or they may specialize in single genera, or groups of them. They often have international appeal, with sister societies in different countries, or with outlying groupings. For example, the Alpine Garden Society, which is based in England, has strong links with the Scottish Rock Garden Club and with the American Rock Garden Society, while maintaining overseas groups under its own aegis in New Zealand, Denmark, Switzerland and Canada among others.

Such societies operate seed exchanges, and their lists are among the most rich veins that the seed-sower can tap. Many of the items will have come from professional or otherwise highly reliable sources, including botanical gardens from all over the world, but a cautionary note needs to be struck, as the majority of the seeds on offer will have come from the gardens of ordinary people who are without botanical or horticultural training.

This does not mean that these lists are full of mistakes, or of offers of bad or misnamed seed. It just means that one should be aware of the fact that some of the items may not be quite what they should be. Anyone taking part in such exchanges should go ahead and order what appeals to them, but the resulting seedlings should be checked over carefully for correspondence with what they are supposed to be.

After all, the possibilities for mistakenness are legion. Firstly, the donor of an item may believe that what he is sending is true to name, but he may be the last link in a long chain of successive recipients of wrongly-named seed, or he might have made an Irish Molly-type blunder, albeit while acting in good faith. Secondly, most plant societies rely upon dedicated amateurs to run and distribute their seed exchanges. They may work in shifts, or the work may be farmed out, but whatever system is used, errors are inevitable, even in the very best-run regimes.

Here, too, one will find many items which are seed from cultivars. There is no harm whatever in having a go with them, but it is futile to hope for more than very ordinary results. It cannot be emphasized too strongly just how widespread and profound is the lack of understanding of the concept of 'not coming true'.

On the other hand, stabilized strains of seed are a different matter. Years of selection will often give rise to plants that come true in successive generations. These are not cultivars and should not be written as such, which is to say with a varietal name between single inverted commas. One such strain is *Digitalis* Mertonensis, which produces plants of a remarkably constant stature and colour—rather like crushed strawberries. It should be written as I have done, without the commas, but unfortunately this practice is rarely followed and the confusion persists. It is much more helpful when identification of a strain is made perfectly clear, as with *Primula pulverulenta* Bartley Strain. This is a strain of primulas whose colour is of a soft, light pink, in contrast to the strong crimson of the species as a whole. A proportion will turn out to be red, and these should be rogued out, or transplanted to a further part of the garden; this proportional reversion happens with seed strains and is something for which to watch out.

Invasive plants

There are among plants, like there are among people, some that are inveterate charmers but which have a capacity for becoming a blasted nuisance. Just to what extent this can happen with plants grown from seed can be illustrated with two personal anecdotes.

A tiny pinch of seed of *Viola macedonica* begged for from a friend in whose garden I saw just one or two plants, promised to provide a delight among alpines. Tiny, but sturdy, and flowering non-stop all season, its dark purple flowers laid a sinister spell upon me. Three years later, it had invaded every nook and cranny of my rock gardens, every choice cushion plant sprouted with the confounded thing, and it even germinated on the dried mud under the wheel arch of an old van. It was never successfully eradicated.

A little charmer, *Sisyrinchium brachypus*, of cheerful mien, with sunny, yellow flowers all summer, and of neat proportions, did precisely the same thing. It must have cost me many hours in weeding time and I grew thoroughly sick of it. It was, however, the subject of a lesson which I have never forgotten, and the object of a deed which I have never repeated. For I confess (and here for the first time after many years) that I pinched the seed while nobody was looking.

Provenance

Strictly speaking, the provenance of seed is a term that refers to its origin in the wild. It is of great importance to foresters who are growing trees for timber. Sitka Spruce, for instance, that originate in British Columbia, will make better timber than those that have their origins in Alaska, because they grow faster and to a greater size.

The provenance of a tree—or other plant for that matter—follows it through its generations away from its place of origin. A Caucasian Wing Nut is still of Caucasian provenance, even if it is a third-generation tree growing in Ireland. If *Magnolia grandiflora* is obtained from Virginia, its provenance is Virginian; if from Seminole County, Florida, then it is Floridian, and both will remain so, no matter where they are grown.

The spread of genera over large tracts of country is of importance to the gardener as well as the forester. *Rhododendron arboreum*, for example, has a wide range of altitudes in which it is happy to grow. At the lower heights of its native range, its flowers are blood red. Higher up, they are pink, and at its highest extent, they are white, or almost so.

It is wise, therefore, for those with colder gardens who wish to grow the species to sow seed from those with the lighter colours, as they will be hardier. In this example it is a relatively easy matter, as the provenance is marked by the flower colour. In other genera one is not usually so fortunate. The fact remains, though, that the provenance can be chosen in cultivation, as it is still the same as it was in the wild.

With *Eucalyptus* the provenance of the seed you sow is very important indeed. A plant from a high altitude will be much hardier than one from lower down, and most species in the genus have considerable altitude ranges. Seed from plants of known provenance, whether in cultivation or collected in the wild, is of great advantage to the eucalypt fancier. It does not matter where the tree is growing at the time of collection, if it is in cultivation. Seed from a Sydney garden may well produce plants that will thrive in London or in Seattle, Washington.

To understand provenance is to cease to fall into one of the more common logical fallacies that holds sway among people—often very intelligent ones—who have to do with plants. Such folk will earnestly tell you that species tend to become hardier as the years pass and as they become acclimatized to a climate that is harsher than their native one.

Successive generations of plants just cannot adapt to alien conditions. To suggest that they can is to imply the inheritance of acquired characteristics, which is a scientific

Dodecatheon meadia will establish happily in a moist, shaded place and is a long-lived perennial.

Primula anisodora is one of the beautiful, moisture-loving candelabra primulas, which germinate well from spring-sown seed that is not covered with compost.

Primula pulverulenta 'Bartley Strain' must be ruthlessly rogued at flowering, those seedlings that show the red of the species being destroyed.

Bupleurums are long-flowering and associate well with shrubs in an informal setting. They are easy from seed and grow anywhere in sun.

It is notoriously difficult to germinate *Acer griseum*, but some success has been achieved by dissecting out the contents of the seeds and sowing them naked.

Camassias grow well in shade and can be readily raised from seed. Sadly out of fashion, they may have their day again.

The enormous flower-heads and large, velvety leaves of *Hydrangea sargentiana* are genetically coded within seeds the size of fine dust particles.

Tree peonies, like *Paeonia lutea* var. *ludlowii*, display double dormancy of the seed. A little patience reaps a large reward.

The seeds of *Enkianthus campanulatus*, a member of the heather family, are not shed until after the shortest day of the year.

heresy. What happens is that less hardy specimens are eliminated, while those that are hardier survive. Even given an element of cross-breeding in cultivation, plants from a hardier provenance will become genetically dominant, it having been the original provenance that allows the species to appear to 'adapt'.

Plant Breeding

It may at first seem contradictory to talk, almost in one breath as it must seem, about the dangers of expecting good results from seed of cultivars and then about breeding plants. After all, by far the greater part of the breeding that goes on uses garden varieties in attempts to improve upon them.

One is, however, talking about two very different things. One is a 'chuck it and chance it' approach to growing garden plants; the other is a deliberate, systematic, planned process which carries in it the germs of success.

There is no doubt at all that the amateur gardener has every chance, if he wishes to pursue it, of creating new garden plants that are superior to those which exist. It may take him a very long time, and he may have innumerable failures on the way, but it is still possible. He may work either with pure species or with cultivars, or with a mixture of the two, but above all he must know what he means by a 'superior' or a 'better' plant. He must be possessed of taste and judgement and of a high degree of objectivity. He must also be so stern of character that he is able to resist naming a plant that does not measure up to the highest standards just because Auntie might mention him in her will if he calls it after her.

That amateurs can succeed—often spectacularly—is well-documented. The Gold Medal-winning rose 'Lincoln Cathedral' was raised by an amateur who had been breeding roses for twenty years. Also amateur-raised was 'Pillar Box', a red rose of such an appropriate colour that its introduction and publicity were sponsored by the British Post Office. There are many more such examples, not all of them on such a grand scale, but all revealing the skill and patience with which the ordinary gardener can rival the professionals.

Lest 'amateur' should be thought of as a pejorative term, I am using it in the strict sense of 'one who does it for its own sake'. The weavers who produced the Paisley Pinks, and the cotton workers who bred the exquisite show auriculas were humble men indeed in their place in society, but their art and their plantsmanship were of the highest order. That they had tiny gardens and very few facilities beyond cold frames heated by horse manure did not deter them from their breeding aspirations, many of which have remained unmatched. How much more so can the modern gardener, with so many more resources available to him, stand with the professionals and beat them at their own game.

It is, of course, useless to dash round the garden with a camel-hair brush, making a noise like a bee. There must be a purpose, an end object in view.

To illustrate this, let me cite the case of *Diascia* 'Ruby Field'. *Diascia* is a South African genus of herbaceous and sub-shrubby plants, whose flowers are in various shades of pink or red, and which have two backward-projecting horns, or spurs, rather like a nemesia.

By sheer luck, there came into my possession in 1970, two species of *Diascia*. *D. cordifolia* was hardy, but its flowers were rather small and of a light red colour. It flowered for a long season, from early summer to early autumn. *D. barberae*, by contrast, was not hardy and had to be kept going by over-wintered cuttings. Its flowers were much larger and of a very pleasant, light salmon-pink. It, too, had a long season of flower.

I decided to attempt to cross them. What I was looking for was a larger flower than in *D. cordifolia*, with a colour more salmon-pink than red, on a plant that was hardy and which would retain the long-flowering of both parents. Anything less would not do, and if I failed to achieve these purposes in this combination, I would either persist until all hope was gone, or give up.

Taking pollen from *D. barberae*, I placed it on the stigma of one flower only of *D. cordifolia*. I did not want the seed-bearing flower to be killed by premature frost, so chose the hardier one as the seed parent. I had not observed either to set seed before, so took no further precautions to prevent pollination from another source.

In due course, this flower and no other, set nine seeds. All germinated, and only two seedlings showed the promise that I was seeking. The other seven were destroyed. One of the two was uprooted by a duck and perished. The other possessed all the qualities that I was looking for, so I sought the permission of Mrs. Field to call it after her, propagated it by cuttings, and put it on the market as a plant for the rock garden or for the front of the border. It is now grown all over the world, where its great flower bearing capacity has made it a favourite.

Of course, it was just luck that allowed one gardener to have specimens of the two species that were available and that they were not readily obtainable. It was also luck that imbued a young nurseryman with the sudden whim to cross the two. Nevertheless, there was a plan and a set purpose, fulfilled, again luckily, at the first attempt.

Given a coherent plan and a sensibly conceived objective, plant-breeding should be carried out with much more rigour than I employed.

Firstly, all precautions should be taken to ensure that the seed-parent flower shall not become infected with pollen from any source other than the one that is in the plan. The flower should be opened just before it is ready to open of its own accord, and the anthers should be removed, leaving the stigma, which should be protected with a paper or muslin bag from the accidental incidence of pollen.

The pollen-parent flower may be introduced once the stigma on the seed parent flower has become sticky at its end. The whole flower may be removed and brought to the scene of the nuptials as soon as the anthers are ripe and are showing free pollen. The anthers are then wiped gently over the stigma of the seed parent flower so that some pollen adheres to it, and the protection replaced. At this stage a label, complete with the details of both parents and the date of the marriage should be attached to the seed parent just below the flower.

When seed is set, it should be sown in the normal way. The seedlings should be planted out in a group, or row, where they can be seen together and compared, and they should not be judged until they have begun to show to the full their qualities as plants and as flowers. Every effort should be taken in trying to persuade oneself that the results are no better than either of the parents; the slightest doubt, and the seedling should be destroyed.

Of course, should you wish to play about to your heart's content and to practise plant-breeding on a large scale, crossing everything in sight and having enormous fun in populating your garden with plants that nobody has ever seen before, then do so. Everyone is entitled to grow just whatever he likes in his garden, as long as it is not a notifiable pernicious weed. Just don't give the plants names or distribute them under such names. Auntie might reward you, but nobody else will.

Sowing the Seed

The conventional way of dealing with seeds of hardy annuals, many vegetables, and trees, is to make a seed-bed out of doors.

Although peas, beans, beets, and so on are best sown in the rows in which they are to grow, there is really little to recommend outdoor sowing. One of the first requirements is a 'fine tilth'—a condition of the soil in which it is broken down and raked to a smooth, flat, just crumbly texture. That this is well-nigh impossible for many gardeners seems to be completely ignored. On clay soils you may have to wait for weeks, especially in a wet season, for the soil to become remotely workable in this way, and you will only have to miss the ideal state by a few hours to find that the sticky stuff has baked to the consistency of granite.

Even if you succeed in getting the bed looking something like it should, it is quite likely that beneath the perfect-looking surface, great lumps lurk, between which are air pockets into which tender new roots will wave in a vain and sad search for sustenance.

No matter how good your soil, disaster will lie in wait for you. Your garden may have soil like black flour, tilled for centuries and manured incessantly; never mind—trouble will not be far away.

A seed bed is sought out by cats much as roadside facilities are eagerly looked for by motorists seeking relief. Birds will bathe in its dustiness with the avidity of tired footballers in their post-match tub. And slugs, wearied of having their bellies scratched by the harshness that surrounds it, will congregate upon its easeful surface, there to find not only a comfortable lodging, but an excellent restaurant as well.

Tree seedlings are particularly vulnerable to weeds, as they grow slowly. To sow tree seeds in a seed bed is to court unending work and disappointment, as the weed seeds, present in great numbers and enjoying the conditions that you have made so good for germination, leap into action with the express intention of throttling the young trees to death. Take a bare piece of soil and then make part of it into a well-prepared seed bed. Wait a week or so and just watch what happens. The seed bed will have by a very long way the richest crop of weeds both in quantity and in variety.

Your painstakingly prepared bed will, of course, develop an impermeable pan as soon as it rains. This will in turn become baked solid by the sun, and further water and, above all, air, will be excluded. The better the tilth, unfortunately, the worse it pans.

It is far better to sow the very great majority of seeds indoors under controlled conditions, where predators can be excluded, weeds can be kept to an acceptable minimum, and the sower's comfort can be very much improved. One of the arguments against this is that some plants *must* be sown where they are to grow, as they hate root disturbance. It is not a good argument, though, as it is a perfectly good practice to sow them just a few in a pot, reduce them to one good seedling, and plant out before the pot becomes too full of roots. If it is ever necessary or desirable to do things to plants that they do not like, the thing is to do it in a manner which prevents them from noticing.

Frames

The simplest 'frame' of all.

An extremely easy frame for the home handyman to construct.

The best place for seeds to be left to get on with the process of germination is in a frame of some sort. Although it is not necessary or even desirable for all kinds of seed, a frame equipped with a method of producing bottom heat is ideal for the great majority.

The frame can be sited in the open, but it is a much better economic proposition, as well as being easier to control, if it sits on the staging of a greenhouse. The heat is much more constant and is not being generated at expense merely to be dissipated directly into the open air.

Criticism is often levelled at gardening writers and broadcasters on the grounds that they tend to describe structures and methods that are beyond the resources of the average person. It is, however, the principle that should be the message, not the detail, and those whose available space and disposable spare cash are limited should find themselves able to sort the pips from the flesh and adapt ideas to their means.

In this case, if there is no greenhouse, so be it. The frame can be insulated in some other way while germination takes place. If it is suggested that more than one frame is of benefit, but there is only room for one, then let one suffice. If bottom heat is too expensive to instal and run, then the position is dire indeed, but all is not lost; a great many seeds will germinate without it, but less efficiently.

The ideal, then, is to have enough frames to contain all the seeds that you want to sow, and that they should be installed within a greenhouse. It is worth bearing in mind that the gardener who is going in for seed in a major way is setting out along a path that will save him a great deal of money that might otherwise have been spent on expensive plants.

Bottom heat can be obtained from soil-heating cables, laid on the bottoms of the frames and covered with a layer of sand. This is the best method, but it implies a certain degree of permanence. If the greenhouse is required for part

Above: this is even easier and can be made very large.

Right: an inexpensive commercially-made frame.

Right: a traditional range of Dutch–light frames.

Above: an up-market commercial frame.

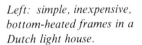

Left: simple, inexpensive, bottom-heated frames in a Dutch light house.

Right: The author's propagating house at Abbotsbury. The seed frames are on the right.

Le dernier cri.

of the year for growing other things, frames with no bottoms can be placed so that they sit on a plastic base which incorporates a recent invention that supplies bottom heat in a most convenient way.

This base has channels within it, in which is a conducting fluid. A small electric current generates an extremely even flow of heat, and the system is very safe. When all germination has been completed, the frames can be removed and stored, and the plastic sheets and their wiring can be simply rolled up and kept somewhere convenient.

Bottom heat does make a great difference to germination rates and to the range of seeds that can be raised. Not only that, it means that seeds can be sown earlier in the year— about seven weeks after the winter solstice.

Most true alpines are better off in a simple cold frame, out in the open and with no heat. The reason is that they need to 'know' that they have experienced a tough winter and that spring has arrived, so an alternation of periods of frost and warming is beneficial. It is a good idea to sow them as early as possible so that this can take place to some effect, and it does no harm at all to take the top off the frame in cold weather, and even to allow snow to fall on the pots of seed. The frame should be closed against rain, which might wash the seeds about, and the ubiquitous cats and other fauna must be guarded against.

Mice are the very devil when seeds are about. They will find their way somehow into the best-constructed frames and greenhouses and if you want to save yourself a lot of heartache, you will have to take precautions against them. Small-mesh welded netting over the tops of frames is a very good idea when the tops are off for letting the weather in, and old structures, which may be made of wood that has developed gaps, will in some cases have to be lined with the stuff. If mice invade greenhouses, you will find yourself with a pair of alternatives when the frames within it are open, or when trays of just-germinated seedlings are standing on the staging. Either you will have to set traps or poison, or you will have to choose between keeping to your humanitarian principles and losing a lot of plants.

Slugs are, of course, a prime source of misery to those who are trying to look after seedlings. They are best dealt with in two stages. Bait should be laid in the frames for a few days before they are used, and any dead slugs picked out. Then the pots should be removed periodically and examined, particularly underneath and beneath their rims, where the beasts are wont to sleep off their gluttony.

If all this sounds like a lot of fuss, then it should be remembered that good gardening is impossible anyway without adequate garden hygiene. This term does not merely include the exclusion of diseases; it also implies the efficient combating of all pests. The definition of a weed is that it is a plant in the wrong place; a pest is an animal in the wrong place. A worm in the garden soil is beneficial; in a seed-tray he is a pest, so the compost you use must be pest-free, too.

Compost

Seed-sowing composts are of two kinds; soil-based and soilless. A soil-based compost can be made up to all kinds of recipes, including the vast majority which are no good at all. The John Innes formula (named for an Institution, not a person—the man involved was a Mr. Lawrence) is now universally used, and it is much better to stick to it than to try to invent something of your own. Plain garden soil is hopeless.

J.I. seed compost consists of two parts by volume of sifted loam, preferably sterilized, one part by volume of sphagnum peat, and one part sharp sand. To this is added 2lb (1kg) of superphosphate and 1lb (0.5kg) of powdered chalk to each cubic yd (0.7 cubic m). It is far, far better to buy this from a reputable source than to try to make it up at home, and it is much cheaper in the long run.

The chalk, of course, renders the compost unsuitable for lime-hating plants, and for these a soilless compost should be used, particularly one which is designated as an 'ericaceous' compost. This term means that it is designed for the family Ericaceae, which includes such things as heathers

65

and rhododendrons, but it is ideal for all plants that will not tolerate lime in the soil.

Soilless composts are made almost entirely of sphagnum peat. There will usually be some sand present, and the nutrient media will have been added artificially.

It is not just the lime-haters that will germinate well in soilless composts. On the contrary, I have found (and others agree with me) that I obtain up to twenty per cent better germination with peat-based composts than with those of John Innes type. They retain moisture at an even rate, while still draining well, and the bottom heat penetrates them better. The one thing that must never happen is that they should be allowed to dry out, because they are impossible to moisten again. Having said that, the seed raiser who allows such a thing to happen is either pretty useless or has been subject to some serious distraction.

Alpines, in fact, do much better on soil-based composts, to which has been added one half of their bulk of sharp grit. They do not (apart from those which are in Ericaceae) appreciate peat composts, and those of them that dislike lime will have to be sown in a soil compost of the grower's own devising. Alpine gardeners are, of course, a law unto themselves and are always concocting composts, so this will be no hardship to them at all.

Weeds—the enemy of the seed-bed sower—are not much of a problem at all with these two kinds of compost, as long as the loam fraction of the soil-based ones is sterilized, as it usually is in good proprietary brands. Some peat composts, though, and this applies, I fear, to those made by the best suppliers, may contain bracken spores. This is a fern of circumpolar distribution and it is a fearful weed which should never come near a garden. Worse, if you are trying to raise fern spores, you will find that the bracken takes over because you have to allow it to get quite big before you can tell it from other ferns.

Sowing

The compost may be contained in pots or trays. Most gardeners, who do not want to end up with vast amounts of plants, will be content with pots that are quite small, but it is a mistake to err too much in this direction. The smaller the pot, the more watering it will need, and therefore the greater will be the variation in the water content of its contents. A minimum of $3\frac{1}{2}$in (9cm) diameter should be aimed for (4in (10cm) is better), and this may be measured from corner to corner if the pots are square.

Square pots are better than round ones because they occupy space more efficiently and the bottom heat does not escape into the air via the spaces that exist between round ones. There is still a disagreement between the proponents

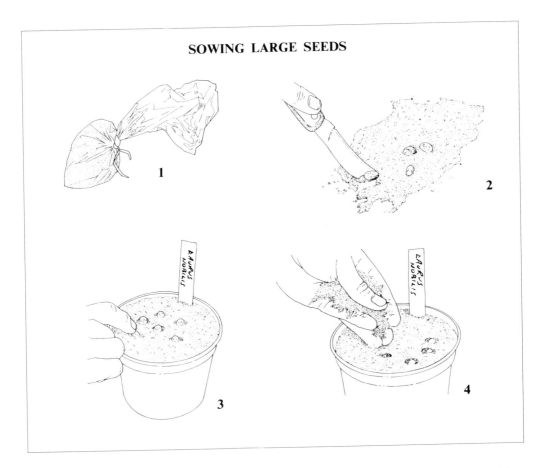

SOWING LARGE SEEDS

Bay tree seed; (1) in moist peat ready for chilling, (2) being sorted from the peat for sowing; (3) large seed like this can be pressed into the surface of the compost and (4) lightly covered. The label should never be forgotten.

Another method of consolidating the compost, using the bottom of a large pot

of plastic and earthen pots, but this should soon be laid to rest, as clay pots become less and less available and more and more expensive. There is something to be said for adding some fine grit to J.I. composts that are made to the traditional formula, as it was devised for clay pots, but peat composts are fine just as they are when used in plastic pots or trays.

It is, too, a mistake to employ too many different sizes of pots. Two or three should be enough, and will make the best and most efficient use of the available frame space. It will also mean that you will not have to have a large battery of differing sizes of compost presses.

I use my hands to load the pots and then to press the compost down and make the surface even, but then I am an essentially lazy and impractical person, not given greatly to woodwork. It is much better to make presses from flat pieces of wood, each with a handle at right angles, with which the compost can be compressed to the right degree and rendered pristine in its flatness of surface. One is made for each size of pot.

I am told that it is much better, but of course have no

DIFFERENT METHODS OF SOWING

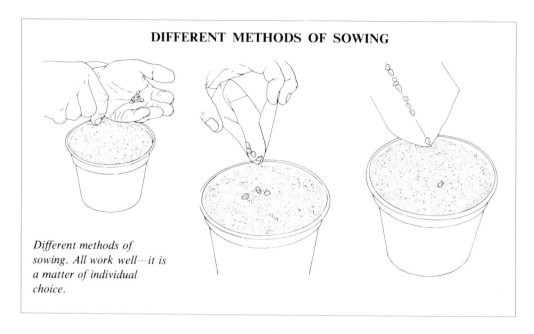

Different methods of sowing. All work well—it is a matter of individual choice.

experience of using such things. What my experience tells me is that my hands can feel lumps and irregularities in the compost and judge the right degree of compression much better than a lump of wood can. That I must be less than well-informed is borne out by the numbers of people who make and use such devices, but I have yet to find one of them whose germination rates are better than mine.

It is, I believe, the current method of choice among the cognoscenti, to tap something when actually sowing the seed. Often it is the seed packet itself that is tapped, or sometimes it is a specially made paper chute. Whatever the vehicle, it appears that to tap ensures even distribution of the seed. I have a little more in common with those who hold the seed in the palm of one hand and tap that hand with the other, as I use my hands myself, but the purpose of the tapping eludes me.

If the seed to be sown is emptied from the packet into the left hand (if one is right-handed), and is then picked up, a pinch at a time, with the tips of the fingers of the right, then the seed can be sown, using a motion rather like the universal sign for money, with considerable economy and perfectly adequate evenness. The sizes of the pinches can be varied at will, and there appears to be a sensitivity inherent in the fingertips that is lacking in paper, no matter how assiduously it is tapped. The palsied trembling induced by last night's wine serves, I find, to assist the distribution rather than to hinder it. Tapping, under such stresses, must surely lose some of its much-vaunted effectiveness.

Be all that as it may, whatever method of sowing is

Sowing a mixture of fine seed and silver sand.

employed should be such that it produces an even distribution of the seed across the surface of the compost, and one that is neither too thick, nor uneconomically thin. Evenness can be ensured with very small seeds by mixing them with a little silver sand and sowing the lot. This will not only dilute the seed; it will also show you where you have been as you sow it.

Seed should be sown, except in the cases of those seeds that should never be covered and those that are very small indeed, so that they are covered by a layer of compost that is no deeper than the width of the seed. This may sound strange when applied to seeds which are flat, but it is still a good rule. Soft, or fragile flat seeds can be sown flat, and then covered with a thin layer of compost; those that are tougher and are quite large can be pushed into the compost edgeways-on, after which a similar layer can be applied. Perhaps 'diameter' is a better word than 'width'—certainly with round seeds, but the principle is the same.

I prefer to use sand as a covering layer for fine seed. Once again, one can see where one has been and this makes for less chance of covering too deeply. What is essential, though, is that the compost used for covering should be dry, or nearly so, as opposed to the compost upon which the seeds are sown, which should be moist, but certainly not wet.

It is advisable with seeds which are not of the smallest sizes to press them gently into the surface of the compost with the palms of the hands. Any that stick can be brushed off the hands, but the process will help to stop the seeds from jumping about as the covering layer is applied. It will, too, play a part in preventing the seeds' being washed about when the pots are watered initially.

There is a great deal of nonsense talked and written about watering newly-sown seeds. That this might add to that body is a risk that must be taken in the interest of expounding from pure experience and not from mere theory.

There are those who insist that peat-based composts should be thoroughly soaked before being put into the pots. Their basis for this is that such composts are difficult to moisten once they have become dry, and this is true. What is silly, though, is to buy peat composts that have been allowed to become dry. Good composts will be nicely moist and they will take up water quickly and efficiently. What is more, wet peat composts are messy to work with and will be deposited into the pots in lumps. Moreover, you have to fill all the pots at once, otherwise you have to wash your hands after each filling and sowing or risk having half the seeds adhere to the peaty mush on your hands, only to find their way into the next batch of totally different seeds. This is probably the rationale behind the tappers—only they never tell you so, as it is a pretty bad one.

A school of gardeners adheres to the method of taking each pot or tray and standing it in a bath of water so that the water gradually rises through the compost. The idea is that the seeds are not washed about, as they might be when a watering-can is used. This is no good at all with peat composts, as the surface peat tends to float, and the seeds with it. It is, however, the method of choice with alpines.

Alpines, germinating as they do to their best advantage in gritty, soil-based composts, do not float off with a layer of compost, especially as it is an excellent practice to cover them with a layer of large grit. This grit—and the very best is the flint grit sold for adding to the feed of turkeys—needs to be put on at between $\frac{1}{4}$ and $\frac{1}{2}$in (60–120cm) deep. Some authorities advocate a depth of an inch (2.5cm), but this tends to produce long, thin seedlings that are not too easy to handle. The lesser depth is ample for its main purpose, which is to stop rainfall disturbing the seeds, and for its subsidiary function, which is to discourage weeds. Some alpine buffs declare that the seed should be sown on to the grit. The idea is that the water, as it recedes, will draw the seeds down into the grit and towards the compost. For sheer idiocy this takes some beating, as it is a palpably inefficient way of putting seeds into the correct germination environment, and a proportion will be immediately doomed to the fate of those biblical seeds that fell upon stony ground.

The watering-can method is decried on two counts. The first is that the seeds become disturbed and their evenness of sowing is lost, and the other is that the compost does not become moistened right through.

On the first count, watering several pots at a time, using a fine rose, and passing the spray back and forth in sweeps, has not disturbed the seed in many thousands of pots and trays that I have sown. Never once have I had the seed washed about so as to induce unevenness of germination. It is, however, essential that the rose be truly a fine one—heavy watering, such as a coarse rose makes inevitable, will fully justify the critics of this method.

On the second, the 'sweeping' method, with several passes over the compost, does indeed ensure that the compost becomes thoroughly moistened, provided that it is not too dry to start with and that the pots are not deep ones. Seed trays and half-pots will be perfectly all right.

One of the worst and most discouraging things that can happen is that a good germination of a treasured subject, just growing away nicely, suddenly starts to collapse. The seedlings will be found limp and fallen over almost as if a lilliputian reaper had taken several vandalistic swipes across the tray. This is damping-off disease, a fungal attack that is fatal and heart-breaking.

The several modern fungicides that are advocated for preventing this malady are severally and collectively of no more value (and possibly of less) than the old-fashioned Cheshunt Compound. This consists of copper sulphate and ammonium carbonate. When hot water is added to it in a small quantity, it dissolves readily with the production of ammonia (so be careful) and is then ready for adding to a much larger volume of cold water. Applied to the pots and trays with the fine-rosed watering-can, just as the very first seedlings are pushing through the soil, it should ensure that there will be no further problem.

Further applications will not harm the seedlings, but should only be used sparingly, if at all. Any damping-off that is resistant to Cheshunt Compound is likely to belong to a group of fungi called *Rhizoctonia*. These are hard to get rid of and can attack other plants, including many vegetables, so sterilization procedures are called for if they occur. They very rarely do, though, so one needs only to know of their existence, rather than to worry about them.

Ferns—a Digression

Ferns are the Cinderellas of gardening. Few nurseries grow them, and rare indeed is the garden centre in whose sales beds they are to be found.

The reasons for this are not difficult to divine. They do not flower, for a start, and in the age in which we live, which is one in which gaudiness, as exemplified by the proverbial 'riot of colour', is the keynote, they have only the tiniest of places. The Victorians loved them, and constructed ferneries, both indoors and out, on the most lavish scales. Those things and values that were beloved in that era seem to be anathema to the people of the late twentieth century, and that is their loss in many ways, although ferneries were, to tell the truth, dull, dismal and damp places.

Monoculture in the ornamental garden is always cloying. Whether it is a vast display of azaleas, from which one soon reels with optical indigestion, a jazz of unrelieved roses, from whose hard tones the eye seeks the blue of the sky for solace, or a depression of ferns, there is no peace to be gained for the senses or for the spirit.

Mix the soft with the hard, the dramatic with the demure, and the loud with the quiet, and one is on one's way to creating harmony. Among the most gentle exponents of the pacific elements of the garden are the ferns, but they need to be part of a composition and not the main subject of a dirge.

Used in this way, as objects of relief to the tired eye and as foci of delicacy, they have a part to play in the garden that, once realized, becomes indispensable. Even so, they may at the same time hold their own in terms of drama. The tree ferns, whose great filigree fronds arch overhead and create jewellery out of the sunlight, and the Royal ferns, stately guardians of the streamside, are not shrinking personalities, but possessors of quiet, regal dignity.

Whoever finally falls for the cheeky greenness of a polypody on a wall, the undamageable glossiness of the Hart's Tongue, or the truly feminine featheriness of the Lady fern, will eventually want to increase his stocks by sowing.

He will sow spores, for ferns have no seeds. They are neuter in gender and do not have organs of sex in the state at which we recognize them as ferns.

For they do, in fact, have two states of existence. The plant which we know as a fern is one generation—the sporophyte, or spore-bearing plant—and it alternates with a generation which does bear sexual organs—the gametophyte, or prothallus.

The alternation of generations is endless, like the conundrum of the chicken and the egg, but we may 'freeze-frame' it at a certain critical stage in order to understand it. On the reverse sides of the fronds of the fern plant (the sporophyte), or in certain plants, on separate fertile fronds, rows of small scales can be seen. These consist of membranes (indusia), covering spore-capsules, called sporangia—a collection of these is a sorus.

Each sporangium produces sixty-four spores in most species, so one does not need very many to give an adequate crop. Their dispersal is highly efficient, so they need to be collected before the sporangia burst. This is best effected by scraping them from the surface of the frond with a knife as soon as one or two have started to disperse their spores. They can then be either sown direct as they are scraped, or collected in a paper bag.

Germination of the spores will give rise to the prothalli, which form a green film on the surface of the compost. This may take up to six months, but is usually much less, and after a few more weeks, the individual prothalli will be distinguishable. The sex cells of the prothalli unite, and from their union grow the young plants of the sporophyte generation, and minute fronds can be seen to develop.

Nature is profligate in the production of the microscopic spores. Well she might be, as very few of them ever germinate in nature. The enemies which they face are legion, and this is just as much so in cultivation, unless we take adequate precautions.

The tiny spores, taking as they do a longish time to germinate, are soon overwhelmed by such things as mosses, and there are sundry creatures that could just do with succulent little mouthfuls of protein. The prothalli are rather like liverworts, and it is just such primitive plants that are likely to supplant them, even if they succeed in being produced in the first place. Moulds, too, are instant death to ferns in their extreme infancy. In short, the soil, or compost, is a death trap, open to a lethally-laden air.

Soil sterilization is, then, essential. It is, however, not difficult. The first essential is a heat-proof pot, which means earthenware or a heat-resistant plastic such as polystyrene. A compost, consisting of one part each of loam, leafmould and sharp sand, or a good clean peat compost in which there are no bracken spores, is placed in the pot and firmed to a level surface. A piece of paper, preferably of the consistency of filter paper, is cut to shape and fitted to come into contact with the surface. Boiling water is then poured over the paper so that it soaks into the compost, and this is continued until the whole, pot and compost, become very hot.

The paper is then removed and immediately a sheet of glass is placed over the pot. When all has become cold again, a few spores—a tiny heap in the tip of a knife-blade—are shaken as evenly as possible over the compost, and the glass is replaced instantly.

The glass should not be removed for watering—this is one discipline in which soaking from below is strongly advocated, and the pots should be placed in a cool, shady place, where the moisture content will vary as little as possible and the condensation on the lower surface of the glass can play its part in keeping the humidity high.

Only when the prothalli have appeared and done their job of initiating young fern plants can the glass be removed and the youngsters pricked out and potted. They will, of course, need to be returned to a close atmosphere until they can be weaned, but the really dangerous phase is over.

Raising ferns from spores is wonderfully satisfying. It is a skilled job, demanding of patience and understanding, and it is one which is rewarded by one's being able to furnish the garden with plants of freshness, daintiness, and sometimes grandeur, which are as long-lived and durable in their adult phase as they are fragile and intensely vulnerable in their reproductive one.

Growing on

Dealing with seeds themselves is a relatively leisurely business. Provided that you do nothing silly, like letting them become damp so that they rot, time is more or less on your side. Harvesting can be frantic, but from then on comes a time for reflection, of studying catalogues, of catching up on one's gardening reading, and of exchanging letters containing fascinating little packets.

Sowing is not too rushed a process, either. A week or so either way is not going to make much difference. Once germination starts, though, a race against time ensues which, if not closely run, is won by nature by a distance.

A frameful of seed trays is something that needs to be examined daily. This is not a chore, but a dip into a box of delights. Bedding dahlias, or *Lupinus arboreus* may be up in a couple of days, while the odd magnolia may appear only after four months. Each day is likely to bring its moment of excitement as minute green studs decorate what yesterday was the same old brown surface.

Once this happens, light and air are the first requirement. The tray or pot should be brought out of its close environment and put on to the greenhouse bench or into another frame, whose lights can be left off in good weather if it is outside. Now is the time when all good slugs are called to the colours and when various predatory insects are lured from their dens to dine destructively upon the delicious morsels that have been served up to them. Cleanliness, neatness, and good garden hygiene are vital to the well-being of the neophytes, and so is a swift scattering of slug bait.

Leave things too long and you will have sickly, twisted individuals that have grown pale and spindly and that will have leaned on one another for support before eventually collapsing in a heap. Let them stay in pots that have not been turned occasionally and the result will be like the staring coat of a wormy horse—all fright-lifted and pointing in one direction. There is no need for a weaning from their amniotic refuge; turn them out and let them get on with life.

The conventional wisdom says that seedlings should be 'pricked out when they show the first pair of true leaves'. Like all aphorisms, this is pithy enough, but is typical of gardening saws in that it does not tell you much. Pricking out is the process of digging the seedlings up and transplanting them elsewhere, but what are true leaves?

What first appear above ground are seed leaves. In the vast majority of cases these bear no resemblance whatever to what leaves of the plants themselves will look like; they are much simpler, more fleshy and, where there are two, they will always be opposite one another. Some seedlings have only one seed leaf.

The flowering plants are divided into those with two, and those with one seed leaf. They are called respectively Dicotyledons and Monocotyledons (a cotyledon is a seed leaf) and these names tend to become shortened to 'Dicots' and 'Monocots'.

The dicots are in the great majority, although grasses are monocots. Most monocots are bulbous or herbaceous, although there are some trees (particularly the palms) among them. *Trillium* is a herbaceous monocot genus; *Yucca* is a woody one. Although there are differences in the veining of the true leaves and in the structure of the wood in each group, what matters to the seed-raising gardener is the differences in the early formations of the seedlings.

With dicots, true leaves will appear in pairs above the seed leaves. The seedlings will have one main root from which other roots will branch; monocots have fibrous roots. Monocots do not produce true leaves in pairs above the cotyledon, but in tufts alongside it.

Our pungent little saying does not apply at all, then, to monocotyledons. If you were a gardener who raised nothing but bulbs from seed, it would not be relevant to any of your plants. What about dicots like heathers and callistemons? Their seedlings are so minute that their first true leaves are quite difficult to see. How on earth do you transplant them at the recommended stage?

The answer is that you do not. The conventional wisdom is, as usual, a load of rubbish, and you prick out all seedlings, whatever their classification, as soon as they can be handled comfortably and without damaging them. Why is it, one wonders, that nonsenses are carried on from generation to generation in the face of all that common sense and practicality have to offer?

Large seedlings can very easily be moved at the two-leaf stage, and here the cotyledons come into their own in practical terms, as they make excellent handles by which to hold the young plants. It is a very bad thing to hold the stems of seedlings, as they bruise at the lightest touch—a bit of a bruise on a cotyledon is something that the seedling can shrug off; damage its stem though, and it is unlikely to recover. Smaller seedlings that are moved when they have several more leaves provide many more handles and they are not likely to suffer stem damage at such a stage.

Some people devise odd instruments with notches in the ends for lifting up seedlings. I tried one once. The trouble was that, when the device was insinuated below the cotyle-

The best method.

dons and lift was then applied, the seed leaves folded up like wings and the seedlings dropped through the notch. No doubt it was my own clumsiness that made me revert to using fingers, but it was certainly rage that propelled the damned thing through the nearest pane of glass.

Nearly all seedlings can be transplanted at times of the year when adult plants would not tolerate it. Some, however, are so susceptible to small amounts of root damage that they are best sown in individual pots and left to grow on in them until they are ready to be potted-on. Magnolias are a case in point. Such seedlings need to be given a feed once they are well-grown but are not ready for the next pot, as the seedling compost in which they are growing is not nutritious enough.

This lack of nutrition is a major reason for the pricking-out of seedlings. Another is, of course, that each individual plant needs room in which to develop.

Small seedlings are, again unlike their elder counterparts, tolerant of a change from a peat compost to a loam-based one. Whereas it is here recommended that peat composts be used at first, the amateur gardener is better off if he has his developing plants growing in a compost made to the John Innes formula for potting. This consists of seven parts by volume of sifted loam to three parts sphagnum peat, two parts sharp sand. To each cubic yard of this is added 2lb of hoof and horn, 2lb of superphosphate, and 1lb of powdered chalk.

The exceptions to this are the lime-haters, particularly those in the family Ericaceae, which in any case are happier in a compost that is thoroughly peaty and which will be going eventually into peaty soils.

The question arises as to why this recommendation to pot into a loam compost rather than a peat one is made when the majority of plants that are bought in garden centres are in containers of peat-based composts. It is a very good question, as the plants are usually excellent, bushy, healthy specimens.

The answer is that it is much more convenient for the nurseries to use such composts. Modern watering techniques suit them, and the plants can be fed regularly and economically and with exactness. The answer is, further, that there are an awful lot of unexplained deaths among plants once they have been planted in ordinary garden soils.

Looking at the first part of the answer, one may justify the recommendation of loam composts by pointing out that the amateur gardener has neither the time, the regulated day, the equipment, nor the inclination to provide the mechanized, routine care that is given by nurserymen, who seek above all to produce a point-of-sale plant as quickly as possible at as high an acceptable price as possible. Slow-release nitrogen, such as is provided by hoof and horn meal, will give rise to a sturdy, solid plant, rather than the sappy, voluptuous, but highly helpless plant that intensive methods produce. Watering does not need to be so critically regular either, which suits people who have to go to work, play the odd round of golf, or go away to visit for the weekend.

The second part of the answer is best illustrated by recalling the disastrous events of some years ago when magnificent plants of a daphne were imported into the United Kingdom from Holland. They all, or very nearly all, died shortly after planting. They had been grown in pure peat and were unable to bridge from it to the loamy soils of the gardens into which they were introduced. So it still is with many garden-centre plants grown in peat composts. After death they will be found, on being dug up, to have no more than their original root ball that they had in the pot. The top will have grown, but the roots will not, thus violating the precept that water lost by the leaf must never exceed that gained by the root. The original peat will be found, as often as not, to be bone dry.

The solution to this problem is to make, not a planting hole, but a planting area, in which the hole is then made. The area should be about a yd (1m) square and should be so cultivated that peat, in generous quantities, is mixed with the existing garden soil to a depth of a spit and a half. If this is done, the roots will make the bridge quite happily. For the home seed-raiser, on the other hand, it is far better to start at the first potting stage with a loam-based compost.

Peat is a godsend to the modern gardener, who is perfectly justified in using it in the relatively minute quantities that are taken up by seed-sowing and by such recherché activities as peat gardening. One day though, sometime in the future, the world is going to wake up to the fact that it is a non-renewable resource, available in a finite quantity, especially in the grades that are suitable for horticulture. Its rapid oxidization on being disturbed results in its disappearance on a scale that is utterly dramatic, and neither oxidized peat nor peat that is extracted from the bog can ever be replaced. There are those who say that the rate of extraction is tiny in relation to the amount available, but that has been said of oil, of whales, of tropical hardwoods . . .

Let us, then, for once fly the flag of soil, even though its weight may reduce the numbers of plants that can be carried on nurserymens' wagons and increase the cost of freighting plants by post or rail. It may even be that, one day, the professional will return to the skills which have been kept alive by the enlightened amateur.

By contrast, the day of the plastic pot is here for as far as one can see. Aesthetics apart (and dirty clay pots are unsightly indeed), there is nothing wrong with plastic. Initial potting should be into a pot that is not too big; 3in (8cm) in diameter is plenty for almost all plants, and potting-on should only be done into pots that are progressively one size bigger than the last. The school that maintains that plastic pots need layers of crocks in their bottoms for drainage is in error. Provided that, when plastic pots are used, the J.I. formula is altered so as to contain more sharp sand, or some grit, there will be no problem. If your compost is well enough drained, then so is the pot. Where water is concerned, what goes up, unless obstructed, must come down.

Towards a Better Garden

The gardener who sets out to grow his garden from seed must learn, if the project is to be successful, the qualities of objectivity and patience, and he must cultivate selectivity to a sensitive and purposeful degree.

Objectivity involves an analysis of what it is he intends to achieve and an accurate viewpoint of how his own activities will either hinder or help in this achievement.

What must always be at the forefront of his mind is that his resources, no matter how adequate they seem to him to be, are essentially limited, and that he must deploy them to the best advantage, not of his ego or of his standing with the neighbours or with the gardening club, but of his garden.

It is not going to benefit his garden if, on receiving 2lb (1kg) of seed of *Acacia dealbata*, he sows the lot, thus preempting himself from using the space for lots of other things, merely to show off his successful technique as he dishes the seedlings out to all his admiring acquaintances. They will not thank him anyway when, ten years later, their 40ft (13m) trees perish in a hard winter, leaving huge gaps in their gardens.

He must, too, endeavour to avoid being caught in the toils of the fashionable. Growing plants from seed is a long-term business, and it is somewhat galling to find that a plant that was fashionable when it was sown now appears to be the monstrosity it has always been. It can be a great investment in time totally wasted when the urge comes upon one to throw out a plant that was *le dernier cri* a decade ago but is now seen as a far cry from attractive.

Crazes, too, are traps for the unobjective. Crazes are, as opposed to fashion, personal obsessions with plants or groups of them. To become fanatical about bulbs at just that time when you found the joys of raising plants from seed could, for example, render you full of bitter regrets when your suddenly jaundiced eye looks out one November day and sees nothing in the garden but bare soil, the odd funereal colchicum, and a landscape like a graveyard for mice—nothing but little headstones with Latin names on them.

The objective seed-raiser will know himself. He will be conscious of the pitfalls of his own personality, and have acquired self-discipline. He will have in his mind a clear idea of the sort of garden that he wants to create, and he will stick to that goal, armed with the other mandatory virtues.

Patience needs no emphasizing. The sort of person who is going to sow seeds rather than spend a fortune on plants has already made a decision that implies patience. There are, however, two kinds of patience. There is that kind that is short-lived and which is allied to that possessed by those who have given up smoking many times, and there is that which is an offshoot of determination and which, dare one say it, is inextricably allied with objectivity.

Growing plants from seed is, except for that part of it that deals with annuals and very fast-growing plants, a slow, long-term business. To obtain a good specimen of the slow-growing *Nothofagus antarctica*, a so-called Southern Beech from Tierra del Fuego, will take many years, but it will be a source of enormous pride and will make a perfect small-garden tree. A seed of the tiny, difficult, alpine cushion plant *Androsace pyrenaica* will take ten years to reach the edges of a 6in (15cm) pot, but what quiet satisfaction greets its award of a first prize on a show bench. There are no short cuts.

Patience is a virtue, and like all virtues it provides its rewards. The gardener who exercises it in his seed-raising activities will experience gratification and profound self-expression on a scale that is totally unknown to those for whom the best gardening tool is a deep purse.

A capacity for selectivity comes with plant knowledge, which in turn is a reward of patience and a product of objectivity. One must know what one is selecting for, both within a species and among species. Am I looking for a shrub that will be attractive when it is out of flower as well as in, or am I looking for a particular kind of ceanothus that will have that quality?

The selective seed-raiser will equip himself with ruthlessness. He will see it as kinder in the long run to rogue out poor seedlings and inferior forms, rather than to let them arrive at maturity before they are cut down in their unsatisfactory prime. It will, too, be kinder to himself. Time, trouble, and precious space will have been saved if the 'eye for a plant' that his knowledge has allowed him to develop has made him able to cast out the lesser things at an early stage.

His objectivity will return to play when he consigns his rejects, not to the garden club plant stall, but to the compost heap or the fire. It is one thing to make a present of a fine seedling to a friend; it is quite another to encourage one's failures to inhabit, or even to infest, the gardens of others. The gardeners with the best reputations have never sought them, but have gained them through recognition of their plantsmanship.

Objectivity, patience, and selectivity will be sternly applied by the gardener who raises new hybrids. Fate will deal severe blows to those who proliferate inferior plants for the sake of recognition, expressed in never-ending litanies of relatives' names. The day will come when certain surnames, or names of houses, will become badges of dishonour, and woe betide the plant, no matter how sublimely and richly superior, that at last emanates from the raisings of such people. One look at the name and the most dispassionate judge will consign it to oblivion with a stroke of a vitriolic pen.

It may seem, then, that the person who seeks to sow a better garden needs to be imbued with the qualities that are sought for in saints and which are seldom found, even among the ranks of the most godly. This is not so, thank goodness. Great plantsmen and women come as rogues, sinners, drunks and bores just as much as any other subdivision of mankind. What they have in common is, simply, a deep and enduring love of plants. It may be because plants do not answer back, run away, or commit betrayal; it may be the product of a simple affection for natural things. It does not matter. The better garden will have been sown with a love that, in some magical and illogical way, feels as though it is returned.

Trees

Much of what has been written about raising trees from seed has emanated from the pens of foresters, as opposed to gardeners, or from those whose management of very broad acres has led them to grow trees on a large scale.

The result of this has been to frighten off the home gardener, who has been led to suppose that forestry techniques—outdoor seed beds and so on—are essential. They are not. Trees can be raised by their being sown in frames and grown on in pots just like anything else, and the seedbed method is quite unnecessary for most of us, as we are not likely to want more than just a few trees in our gardens.

Even if, as I do, you garden on a large scale and sell quite a lot of trees, there is no reason in the world why you should not sow them in controlled conditions and grow them in pots. The only proviso is that a close watch should be kept on them so that they are potted-on well before their roots have a chance to curl up upon themselves and become solid masses that will resist being persuaded to grow properly.

A very high proportion of tree seeds can be sown in the early spring in bottom heat and without any previous treatment. Some, which comes from cold climates, may well benefit from being subject to alternating periods of chilling and warming before they are sown, but even these can surprise with the readiness with which they germinate without. It is a good idea, however, to split batches of such seeds into halves and to give one the cold treatment, while leaving the other for direct sowing later.

Some of the birches are best treated in this way. *Betula papyrifera*, the Paper Birch, has a range that extends from Nebraska to Hudson's Bay, and it was used for making canoes. Seed from Warren County, New York, reached me two years running. In the first year, both half-batches germinated extremely well, but in the second, only the pre-chilled seed came up, while just a couple of seedlings emerged from the later-sown half. Because we are unlikely to want more than a few seedlings to grow on, it does not represent such a great loss if half the seed comes to nothing. It might, in fact, be either half, but it is unlikely to be both.

It is a very sensible attitude to take that suggests that 'experts' and writers (this one included) often talk a lot of nonsense. It is, for instance, stated categorically somewhere—I forget where, but it is an 'authoritative' source—that *Sophora tetraptera* must have its seed soaked in boiling water or be subjected to abrasion if it is to germinate at all. This lovely small to medium-sized tree is one of the gems of the New Zealand flora and any effort is worth while if it is to grace one's garden. Being possessed of a sceptical and untrusting nature, and having been sent a large quantity of seed from each of two wild stands of the tree by a friend who was in New Zealand, I set up an experiment.

One hundred and fifty seeds were taken from each gathering and split into fifties, one of which was treated with boiling water, one by abrasion, and to the last nothing was done at all.

The three hundred seeds were sown on the same day in the same compost and were placed in the same frame. Germination occurred after five weeks and was regarded as complete after seven. The germination rate was between forty-three and forty-eight out of fifty in every one of the six batches. No difference. Q.E.D.

Gardeners are also put off by the quite understandable feeling that trees are too long-term a proposition to be grown from seed at home. There is a lot of truth in this, but there are a great many trees that are fast-growing in their early years but which never become really big.

Acacia dealbata, the Mimosa of florists, can attain a height of 40ft (13m) in less than ten years from sowing. This is a tree that can be grown wherever frosts are not severe, and particularly where it is sheltered from wind-chill factors. Its delicate, filigree, grey-green foliage is present all the year round, and its myriads of lemony-yellow pom-poms are one of the greatest possible delights of the very early spring.

In complete contrast, and for that reason an ideal companion for the Mimosa, is *Idesia polycarpa*. This has large, broad leaves with bright red petioles and red veining. It will be 5ft (1.5m) high after two years, and will be a noticeable tree after about seven. Although you need a male and female if you are to see the red fruit, the foliage and habit of the tree—it is deciduous—make it a great asset. It is an example of a species in which provenance is important, as some forms are very hardy, while others are less so.

In the genus *Acer* there are some fast growers, as well as some very slow ones. *A. pensylvanicum*, grown for its beautiful green-and-white striated, 'snakebark' stem and for its autumn colour, will make its mark on the garden after seven years or so, while *A. flabellatum* var. *yunnanense*, whose leaves are extremely lovely, can put on well over 2ft (60cm) a year in height in its youth. Both are hardy trees.

The champions in the speed stakes are the eucalypts. Unlike the other trees mentioned above, many of them can become really large in time, but *Eucalyptus* is a very strange genus indeed, to which few rules apply, and one of their idiosyncrasies is that they can be reduced in height by any amount and take no harm from it.

Provenance is, as we have seen in a previous chapter, of the first importance with this Australian genus. The increasing use of seed from hardy provenances has had the result of making discussion of eucalypts much less academic for those who garden in frosty climates, and there is now a range of a dozen or so species that can be grown in places that are really quite cold in winter. The sub-tropical, highly exotic look that they give to the garden is belied in a way in that temperatures as low as minus 12°C can be tolerated by them for a few days at a time, even with an element of wind-chill on top of that.

To illustrate their rates of growth, it can be mentioned that *E. nitens* has attained 20ft (6m) in five years, *E. viminalis* the same height in four, and *E. coccifera* is a mighty tree of 60ft (20m) after twenty years. This is hardly short-term gardening, and for those with small gardens there are small eucalypts which do not grow much bigger than the average medium-sized shrub, but which get there quickly.

Much claptrap is talked about the raising of eucalypts. There is, once and for all, no need to set fire to the seed in order to make it germinate! Almost all the species will come up like cress if they are sown on to the surface of a peat-based compost and left uncovered, save for a little sand over the larger seeds of the tropical species. Bottom heat is just about essential, however, but further mumbo-jumbo is not required.

Much wisdom is, on the other hand, distilled into the Australian saying that the taller the stake, the taller will be the eucalypt when it falls down. Eucalypts are very difficult to make wind-firm, and the worst thing to do is to stake them; the second worst is to give them any manure at all. They should, if sown in the very early spring, be planted out in the middle of the same summer. They may only be 8in (20cm) or so tall, but this does not matter; they will quickly make straight trees that will stand the wind and will not have to be subjected to the alternative treatment, which is to cut them right down to ground level and start again—a waste of time if ever there was one.

Eucalypts are examples of trees that look good at all times of the year. Their blue-green foliage (which may tend more to blue or more to green according to species) is quite different from anything else, and is always striking, whether in the rounded juvenile stage or in the more or less sickle-shaped adult one.

The average garden does not have room for many trees, so it is a pity if those that are grown do not share this all-year-round attractiveness. There are so many that do that there is really little excuse for not using them.

Betula albo-sinensis septentrionalis is a delightful little birch with airy foliage that glows bright gold in autumn. In winter its bark is one of the glories in the garden, especially when the sun glints through its light, pink-orange, peeling bark. How much better this subtle magician pays its rent than does the wildly over-planted *Robinia pseudoacacia* 'Frisia', whose strident, shrill yellow screams from every suburban corner! It does sometimes set viable seed in cultivation, and it is worth every effort to obtain.

Acer griseum is another small tree with peeling bark, only with this one it is mahogany in colour, glowing with the richness of old vintage port when struck by the sun. Seed is set, but is notoriously difficult to germinate. Success has been attained by carefully dissecting out the embryo and associated tissues from the seed coat and sowing it naked. It is, again, well worth the effort, and is certainly a better proposition than paying a fortune for somebody else's achievement.

By no means all worthwhile trees with year-round appeal are difficult to obtain as seed or to germinate. *Betula maximowicziana* is far more hard to say than to find; it germinates easily, and has very nice, orange bark that turns white. *Acer circinatum* is equally easy and has foliage that is delicately tinted in early summer, but flamingly red and orange in autumn. It is also highly decorative in its flowers which are shown off by bright red bud-scales. These two trees, planted near to each other, make a harmonious and complementary pair.

It is truly a great shame if the would-be raiser of tree seeds is put off by any of the apparently discouraging factors that occur to him. He is, for one thing, missing the opportunity to be one up on the person who thinks himself no end of a propagator because he does everything from cuttings. It is, frankly, impossible to raise eucalypts from cuttings, as it is with palms, and the Judas Tree, *Cercis siliquastrum*, can only be obtained from seed. It is pointless to try cuttings of the Foxglove Tree, *Paulownia tomentosa*, because 20ft (6m), flowering trees are growable in groves in seven years, and there is a whole host of rarities that cannot be found except as seed.

As the society in which we live has tended to become more and more a mobile one, gardening has veered away from being concerned with the long-term and has taken on connotations of the instant and the here-and-now. This is one of horticulture's tragedies. It is perfectly easy to understand the upwardly-mobile family who must move where the job takes them and the growing family who seek to improve their housing standards. They are unlikely to want to invest too much in terms of time and emotion in seeing trees through from the seed packet to late adolescence, only to have to abandon them to the next owner. The new garden is unlikely to find them wanting to repeat the experience, and by the time they reach their last home, they are probably considering the span of years left to them as being insufficient for the raising of trees to be worthwhile.

Sales of property can be arranged, however, so that trees can be moved. It is, of course, much better to foresee one's home move some time ahead so that preparations can be made and the move made during the winter, but this is not always possible. Failing this, it may be possible for the new owner to allow the moving of trees after the property has changed hands, but this must be cut and dried at the time of sale.

With a few exceptions—magnolias, *Cornus*, *Eucryphia*, *Eucalyptus* and *Cercis* are among them—trees of up to ten or twelve years old can be moved quite easily during quiet, unfrosty weather after the fall and before new growth starts in the spring.

If possible, a circular trench should be made round the trunk a year before. This should be about a spit deep and any large roots are cut. It is done during the dormant season and its purpose is to promote fibrous root growth during the coming growing season. The trench will be at a different distance from the trunk with age of the tree—as a rough guide, a 10ft (3m) tree will have the cut made at about a 2ft (60cm) radius from the trunk.

The following year, the tree is lifted, starting with a re-digging of the trench, and with as much soil adhering to the roots as possible. The roots can be wrapped in canvas or hessian, and the tree moved as quickly as possible to its new site. If the move of the tree can be integrated with the moving of the household effects, so much the better. It can be a prohibitive expense to pay for the transport of just a couple of trees over a considerable distance.

On the other hand, a garden furnished with a few really good young trees, well-grown and exhibiting attractive characteristics at whatever time a prospective buyer might view the property, cannot but increase the value of the place or, at the very least, be the clincher for a wavering pur-chaser. It may be totally impossible to take them with you, but you can dry your eyes in the knowledge that they have paid their way.

Conifers

Whenever thoughts turn to plants that are good-looking throughout the year, conifers spring to mind. That they spring to some minds more readily than to others is because they are subjects both of fashion and of crazes.

Conifers are fashionable because the garden centres are

full of them and because they are nearly all hardy and very easy to grow. A particular fashion has caught on with gardeners who have acid soils—that of the conifer-and-heather garden. The idea is that you have colour of flower and foliage all the year round combined with great ease of maintenance, involving as it does a weed-free environment. The fact that the end result looks perfectly ghastly has not deterred it from being seen in the most hideously inappropriate settings and repeated *ad nauseam* in places where petunias and stocks would be much nicer.

They are the subject of a craze because they appeal to the mentality of the collector. There is a mystique about their names that renders him who can manage them one up on his neighbour. If you can reel off *Chamaecyparis pisifera* 'Plumosa Compressa' at the local produce show they will think you no end of an expert. No end of a bore, as well.

Dwarf conifer buffs have peer-group-acceptance habits. They will take a handful of foliage and half pull, half stroke it from base to apex, while at the same time protruding the upper lip and knitting the brow sagely before announcing that it is not the *true* whatever-it-is, as they have the only specimen in cultivation.

Thank heaven, the sower of a better garden cannot really be a dwarf conifer addict, because dwarf conifers are cultivars and do not come true from seed. Coloured forms of large ones do not either, for the same reason. Should he, then, garden without conifers?

Certainly not. There are several conifers, including some exquisite beauties, that will provide him with plants of architectural excellence and importance, as well as first-class all-year-round appeal.

Picea brewerana, for instance, is one of the most breathtakingly beautiful of all small to medium-sized trees. It is conical in shape, but in layers of spreading branches, from which hang slender, wispy branchlets like Spanish Moss. No description of it will ever better that in Hillier's *Manual of Trees and Shrubs*: '... this spruce with its curtained branches, rising like a majestic green fountain.'

Seed, sown in the early spring, either with bottom heat or in a cold frame, will germinate readily, but it is something of a long-term job to obtain a really fine specimen. What rewards await those with the patience to see the splendid results!

Among the smaller species conifers, the Korean Fir, *Abies koreana*, is a winner, inasmuch as it produces its violet-purple, conspicuous, upright cones very early in its life. It is an adult, well-formed tree at 6ft (2m) tall and does not take many years to attain that height. Both this and Brewer's Weeping Spruce are perfect lawn specimens, where

Using *Diascia barberae*, a tender species, as seed parent, the author performed the cross with the much hardier *D. cordifolia* to produce *D.* 'Ruby Field', an improvement on both.

Sterilized soil, coolness, and a covering to keep out alien spores are necessary for raising ferns like *Matteuccia struthiopteris*, the shuttlecock fern.

The yellow, scented azalea, *Rhododendron luteum*, can be grown in drifts at low cost if grown from seed.

Some of the greatest satisfaction in gardening can come from raising trees from seed. *Betula utilis* displays its snowy bark.

A fine hybrid rhododendron, raised from sed and as yet un-named.

The form of *Celmisia coriacea* from Secretary Island in the far south of New Zealand germinates far better than any other and was worth the long journey to find.

Salvia argentea is a biennial. It makes its growth in one year and flowers, sets seed and dies in the next. It is very easily kept going from seed.

Ramonda myconii, a shade-loving Pyrenean alpine, whose tiny seedlings need careful handling and whose seed should be sown on the surface of a peaty compost.

their deep green colourings are set off perfectly by the lighter green of the grass, and where their shapes and the details of their foliage and fruit are not subject to distraction from neighbouring plants.

There are several really interesting conifers that are not common in gardens and that have that indefinable quality of 'character'. They are almost never seen in garden centres, but their seed is offered fairly regularly in specialist lists.

Among them is *Cunninghamia lanceolata*, the Chinese Fir, a tree that looks for all the world as though it should be tender, and yet its tropical appearance is combined with hardiness as long as it is not subject to strong winds. *Cupressus funebris* and *C. cashmeriana* are two more beautiful, weeping, small trees (the latter is tender), while *Pinus pumila* is a true dwarf species, suitable for the rock garden, and quite different from the oddities and horticultural lap-dogs of the conifer fancy.

Shrubs

Shrubs are the stock-in-trade of garden centres. They make, for the most part, good, saleable plants quickly, and there is a reasonably wide variety of shrubs that are easy to grow in almost any soil and in most climates. They are a long-term proposition in the garden and suppress weeds. They need no staking or cutting-back each year, they are more disease-free than most groups of plants, and they do not have to be lifted and divided from time to time as herbaceous plants do.

Why not, then, go along to a few garden centres and buy the shrubs you want? Well, a lot of people do, but, as we have seen previously, they are all likely to end up with gardens that are stocked with much the same things, good though they may be. It also costs a good deal of money to indulge in off-the-shelf gardening, and the seed-raising gardener will be looking to have a garden that is different as well as one that is set up at less cost.

He will be well advised to buy such things as camellias, evergreen azaleas and shrub roses, as he will be unable to compete with the excellence of the varieties that have been raised over centuries, but there is an enormous range of other things that are just as good, if not better, from seed. Not only that, but he can experiment with plants that would be a doubtful investment if they are considered not to be hardy in the area in which he is gardening.

Then, too, he will be able to consider planting shrubs in groups, or even in drifts. So many shrubby gardens are spotty, with a single specimen of this here and that there. A packet of seed, even of a difficult subject, will be likely to produce three or four plants at the very minimum, and much more natural and pleasing effects can be obtained.

The yellow scented azalea (*Rhododendron luteum*, but often sold as 'Azalea pontica'), is not often offered for sale as plants, and when it is the price is likely to be rather high. It is easy from seed, although it takes a few years before the plants make substantial shrubs, and it is one that really should be grown in groups. The scent in spring is truly wonderful, the colour of the flowers is a clear, soft yellow, and the foliage is very attractive even before it turns to dazzling red in the autumn.

Sown in the early spring—not in the autumn, because the seedlings are so small at first that they are hard to look after during the winter—it germinates easily on the surface of a peat-based compost that has had no lime added to it. It is always possible that a bit of cross-pollination may have taken place if other deciduous azaleas have been grown with it, but selections can be made when they first flower so that those that have the typical flower of the species are retained. The others are likely to be good plants, too, so they are worth hanging on to to give away or to plant elsewhere in the garden.

Other species azaleas, such as *R. schlippenbachii* and *R. vaseyi* are good value from seed, while *R. occidentale* is one that flowers later than the others and extends the azalea season. This species had been the subject of some excellent work in the United States in recent years, in which it has been successfully crossed with other species, such as *R. viscosum*, to give us late-flowering deciduous azaleas in which scent and delicate colours have been combined to great effect. There is really no reason why this field should not be entered by amateur gardeners. There is almost no such thing as a bad deciduous azalea, and the home gardener who uses sense and selectivity could quite readily come up with something all of his own and very good indeed.

Not only does a group or drift of *Rhododendron luteum* make a delightful picture in the garden; groups of the others do as well. I have yet (I think) to see a really vile clash of colours among these azaleas, even though their hues are strong, but groups can be planted so that colours grade into one another, with white used as a buffer where necessary. Japanese, or evergreen azaleas can clash badly both among themselves and with the deciduous ones. Nothing looks worse than the purple-mauve tones of the Japanese azalea 'Atalanta' next to a deciduous azalea in the 'Hotspur' range of orange. There is really no point in trying to avoid buying varieties of Japanese azaleas; they set no seed anyway in cool gardens, and the results would be dubious, to say the least.

For those who like the style of foliage of rhododendrons but who have limy soils, skimmias are readily grown. Their bright red fruits contain viable seeds that germinate with little effort, but they produce plants of different sexes. The flowers of skimmias are lightly scented, and their evergreen foliage is an asset, but you will have to plant a group of them if you want to have berries. Four or five should be enough for chance to provide at least one and probably two females.

On the other hand, experience triumphs over received information in the case of *Callicarpa*. This, in the form of the species *C. bodinieri* var. *giraldii*, is a highly unusual shrub in that its flowers and berries are of the same colour, a metallic violet that is unmatched by anything else. The flowers are borne in late summer and the berries in autumn, and these last for a long period into the winter. Everyone says that you need two or three to obtain berries, but I have one that fruits prolifically every year and I know for certain that there is no other specimen within a radius of five miles. The point is that the colour is so outstanding and unique, as well as being so strong, that just one plant is enough in most gardens and a drift is too much of a good thing. It should be noted that it is very hardy, but the almost identical *C. americana* is tender. It is truly remarkable that the two species, one from China and the other from the forest floor in the deep south of the USA should be so alike in appearance. That they must have belonged to the same species before North America broke away from Asia and turned upside down puts the time-frame of evolution into perspective. Each, too, has the quality of quenching thirst if just one berry is sucked for a while. I have tried it with both, and it works for me just as it did for the native Americans of Florida.

Eucryphia is another genus that has split into two as the continents have separated. Three species occur in Australia and two in Chile. The two Chilean species have been hybridized to produce *Eucryphia* × *nymansensis*, of which the best and by far the most usually grown form is 'Nyman-say', the pronunciation of which is indicated by its originally having been distinguished as 'Nymans A.' in contrast to 'Nymans B.'.

This hybrid is, of course, only obtainable as plants or as cuttings, but this does not mean that the genus is closed to those who would like to grow it from seed. 'Nymansay' is, in fact, too large for small gardens. It will grow to well over 30ft (10m) tall and its short flowering period at the end of summer is not enough to compensate for its rather dull, rigid foliage that has to be lived with for the rest of the year. Its Australian cousin, *E. lucida* is a different proposition altogether and comes quite easily from seed.

This is one of the more daintily elegant of evergreen shrubs and it is, moreover, hardy once it has got through its first few winters with a little protection. In contrast to the popular 'Nymansay', its foliage is glossy, simple and dense, and its flowers are white and fragrant. It is a large enough shrub, but takes some years to reach 10ft (3m), at which size it is of great ornamental value. Seed is quite regularly offered and it germinates with little difficulty in quite normal conditions, although bottom heat tends to increase its not very high germination rate. Eucryphias are sensitive to root disturbance and should be handled gently at all stages in their growing-on.

E. lucida is very rarely to be seen in garden centres or nurseries, and it is an example of a plant that is much more likely to be found in the gardens of those who have raised it from seed. It is, too, an instance of selectivity and taste being exercised where it is grown, as it is so much more aristocratic a shrub than the more usually seen eucryphias.

It is a Tasmanian, and it is among the plants from that island and from Australia as a whole that some of the most rewarding opportunities come for experimentation with things that may be rather tender for our gardens but which we just might get away with.

The Australian shrubby flora has produced so many surprises in terms of what will grow in gardens that were previously considered too cold that there is a very considerable traffic of seed from Australia to other countries. The Society for Growing Australian Plants has State branches, membership of which is open to people overseas, and these publish annual seed lists. The top-of-the-tree seedsmen now list numbers of Australian species that would have been unimaginable not so many years ago, and the fact that they find it worthwhile to continue to do so is indicative of the success that their customers have had in raising and growing the plants.

I have already mentioned my consistent failure with the Tasmanian Waratah, *Telopea truncata*, due to unfilled seed. Good seed is now more readily available, and this cousin of the South American *Embothrium* is gradually proving itself hardy in all but the most chilly places. What is even more remarkable is that expert cultivators are gradually finding that other species of *Telopea*, one or two of which have hardly ever been grown in cool temperate countries, can stand up to winters in which temperatures of $-8°C$ are liable to occur. That this genus needs a lime-free soil and dappled shade is something that may have escaped the notice of those who have been less than successful with it in the past.

The bottlebrushes, *Callistemon* species, have been preeminent in astonishing gardeners where frosts are common. Their most attractive, sharply linear foliage appears in the mass rather like a stand of some sort of simple fern, and the brightness of their extraordinary flower-clusters, in which scarlet and crimson stamens radiate round the stems exactly like the brushes that bottles are washed with, is especially valuable as it occurs in mid-summer.

They are sensitive to wind-chill but will almost all tolerate really severe frosts over quite long periods provided that they are in shelter. These are, above all, plants for growing in groups or drifts as large as space can possibly allow. The seed is tiny and germination is easy and generous, so one packet will give you more than enough plants for yourself and for friends.

New Zealand has also much to offer the adventurous

gardener who is prepared to find out how far he can go with plants at the margin of hardiness. *Pittosporum* is a genus of large shrubs, some of which, particularly *P.tenuifolium*, are delighted in by flower arrangers. It occurs mainly in New Zealand, but has outliers as far away as China. The sticky, black seeds are distributed most efficiently by birds, to whose beaks they adhere rather in the manner of mistletoe berries, but their very stickiness makes them quite easy to harvest, as they stay for a long time in their pods after splitting has occurred.

These shrubs are some of the most pleasing of foliage plants and, again with shelter from cold winds, they may well be found to be a lot hardier than was previously supposed.

P.tobira is a pittosporum from Japan and China. It has large, glossy leaves and its flowers, formed in mid-summer, are large and creamy-white and bear a scent that is very similar to orange-blossom. It is readily raised from seed, and it is a good idea to do so, as the shrub is subject to a wilting disease that kills it off in a couple of seasons. The plant, weakened by this, becomes very susceptible to frost and is likely to succumb after a cold winter, leading us to think that it is more tender than it really is. Enough plants, raised from seed, will allow the gardener to try it in different places, thus allowing the chance of finding a spot where it will find a microclimate to its taste and also of growing some that will escape the wilt. The variegated form is indeed tender; it really comes into its own as hedging in southern Europe and the south of the USA, and it has to be raised from cuttings anyway.

It was from the Far East, particularly China, that so many of our finest garden plants originally came. Today there is a new influx of introductions which will reach involved gardeners in the form of seed and among them are some of the choicest plants for the future. It will be a very long time indeed before these become stock lines in the garden centres and the skills of amateur gardeners need to be harnessed as well as those of professionals in their initial establishment. There are many shrubs among the new additions to our garden flora and it is quite possible for one reason or another that they may fail to set seed in cultivation. There may, therefore be only the one chance to raise them from seed, so every chance should be given to the seeds to produce as many plants as possible. I usually split the seed into two halves and sow one in the autumn and one in the early spring, and I keep records of everything that happens, including total failure.

The raising of shrubs from seed is not by any means confined to the upper-crust gardener who wants to experiment with hardiness and try his hand at sampling the product of plant-hunting expeditions. These are activities of the utmost importance for ornamental horticulture and are pastimes from which deep and lasting satisfaction is to be obtained, but they are not for everyone—some of us just want to garden!

There are plenty of thoroughly hardy, reliable, grow-anywhere shrubs that come readily from seed and save the gardener a lot of money in so doing. What could be more lovely, for example, than *Kolkwitsia amabilis*? Its other name, Beauty Bush, is eloquent enough in describing its charms, and its soft pink flowers, massed on the plants in late spring and early summer, never pall even though they may be seen in a thousand gardens. And who, once they have tried it, could be without the supremely easy tree lupin? Good-natured, fast-growing, and generous with its flowers, its short life span is more than made up for by the reckless speed with which it germinates. The gardener who fails to germinate *Lupinus arboreus* is, I fear, either a sublime idiot or is intrinsically poisonous to plants. If, forty-eight hours after sowing in the most inexpert and haphazard manner, there is not the most exuberant germination possible, something is terribly wrong.

No matter, though, whether the plants you have raised are rare and new or quite ordinary, a bit of a trap lies in wait for the raiser of seedlings. The garden-centre buyer gains some idea of the ultimate size, shape and habit of his plants—he is seeing them at a stage when the differences between them are becoming more or less obvious, they are likely to be well-known to him already, and if they are not he has usually only to ask the staff to find out what the plant will eventually be like.

The seed raiser has very often to rely on his own research. If, for instance, he wants to grow a hydrangea from seed, it is as well that he knows that *H.sargentiana* is likely to grow to be at least 10ft (3m) tall. It would look pretty silly if he planted it as a 10in (25cm) youngster alongside a plant of the same size that was only going to reach 3ft (1m) unless he was aware of the discrepancy and had planned for it.

It is a fact of life that all seedlings are small and do not give much of a clue as to their adult dimensions or general appearance. Young seedlings of the weeping bottlebrush do not weep, and some of the willows hide their propensity for growing like Gargantua. The seed-raiser must do his homework.

He must, too, steel himself to ruthlessness and throw out any seedlings that show signs of being runts or that are of poor form for the species. In almost every batch of seedlings there will be atypical specimens and the bad ones must be got rid of, even though there may be very few to choose from. Similarly, any that show promise of special talent should be encouraged as much as possible. Shrubs are around for a long time in the garden and they leave nasty gaps if they have to be discarded at a later date; it is far better to study the batches of seedlings carefully when they are young and select the best ones for the job.

In every garden you are likely to visit that is owned by an inveterate raiser of seed you will find at least one ghastly mistake that has been due to a lost label. The typical sort of thing is a sorbus with red berries where it was intended to plant one with white. Whole planting schemes, especially those based on colour themes can be ruined in this way, as shrubs and trees have to reach a considerable age and size compared with herbaceous plants before they show their true colours. It takes a very strong personality indeed to dig up and remove a plant that is approaching maturity and that has been nurtured all the way from the seedling stage, and such mistakes are more often than not left out of kindness.

With shrub seed and with that of trees, then, labelling is all-important. They are going to be around for rather a long time in trays and then in pots and the labels must not fade in sunlight nor be washed clean by rain. Neither must they be pulled out by birds nor investigated by small children. The seed tray is safest with two labels, one at each end, and every plant in each batch should have its own label. Imagine being rung up by Kew or the Arnold Arboretum who want to know how your sowing of the ultimate rarity is getting along because theirs has failed. 'Oh', you mumble, 'I'm afraid I lost the label!'

Perennials

Strictly speaking, a perennial plant is one that lives for many years. This definition has become restricted over the years so that it has come to apply just to those plants that have soft top growth and die down every winter—in other words, the herbaceous perennials.

Elsewhere, for the sake of clarity but not accuracy, I have used the term 'evergreen herbaceous plants' to describe those that do not die down for the winter; they should really be called evergreen perennials. What a confusing world it is! The tangle can be unravelled by our understanding the contra-distinctions that gardeners have tried to make— between woody and non-woody plants on the one hand and between annuals and long-lived plants on the other.

Perennials, as we are to understand them, do not include bulbs, among which are some of the most soundly perennial of all plants, and neither do they encompass alpines, some of which are really perennials on a small scale. What we are talking about are the herbaceous plants of the border and the evergreen, non-woody plants that tend to be classified either with shrubs or with herbaceous plants, depending upon which book you read.

The border, however, is a nebulous concept. Many perennials grow in places that are nothing at all like the conventional flower bed (the difference between a bed and a border is a valid distinction, but let us not split too many hairs at once). Primulas, for instance, particularly the Asiatic kinds, look at their very best when growing in wide drifts in informal plantings where the soil is really moist. They may grow in combination with shrubs, such as the smaller rhododendrons and azaleas, and other perennials, like *Meconopsis* and *Nomocharis*.

Such a woodland setting is one of the finest for plantings of perennials and there is no alternative to seed-raising for the proper furnishing of such a place other than spending an untold fortune on plants. Some plants, such as the hostas, are obtainable in their most interesting varieties only as plants, but seed of the species is available, and quickly provides plants that make very fine, architectural additions to the woodland scene.

'Woodland' immediately makes people think of gardening on a large scale. It need not, as a small patch of ground beneath and around just a very few small trees can provide conditions that are just as ideal as those in an oak wood. One of the finest woodland plantings that I have seen occupied an area of no more than 15 × 8ft (5 × 2.5m). It contained a wealth of species and the main weeds were self-sown seedlings of the inhabitants.

The largest herbaceous perennial of all is *Gunnera manicata*, from the jungles of southern Brazil. It is sometimes called Giant Rhubarb although, while it is certainly a giant, it is not related at all to rhubarb. In a wet, or really moist soil, its massive roots will thrust leaf-stalks 7 or 8ft (2.5m) into the air, upon which the huge, bristly leaves, like the ears of mastodons, unfold and expand to become as wide as the stems are long. In a woodland where there is a stream, or just a place that is wet, this massive plant creates a mood all by itself and suggests the darkly primitive when its peculiar, club-like inflorescences arise like furled besoms beneath the expanses of green leather.

It sets seed all right, but what a fuss is necessary to get it to germinate! (See page 30.) Once the seed is up there is no longer any need for further antics and the young monsters can be potted up and started on their very long lives.

Gunnera is not tender, but it does not appreciate really cold places either. Where it is cold, or where there is not room for such a Brobdingnagian element, true rhubarb will give a junior version of the same effect. *Rheum palmatum* is one of the species and, in the form 'Bowles's Purple', whose leaves are reddish-purple underneath, it is very fine. From seed, though, you will get green-leaved forms, but they are almost as good. The Greeks knew two plants called *Rha*; the *Rha ponticum* from the Pontus and *Rha barbarum*—the Rha of the barbarians, from which we get 'rhubarb'. It may seem a touch barbaric to grow rhubarb in your informal plantings, but just wait until the fashion for bedding-out ornamental cabbages and kales gets going!

If the large, leafy plants are the furniture of the woodland garden, primulas form the carpet, certainly in the spring and the early summer. There are a great many species of Asiatic primulas, but those that are reliable for the majority of climates and gardens are few. As a whole, they demand coolness as well as moisture, and the climate of Scotland is the sort that suits them. Luckily for us who live where summer can be hot and winter cold, those species that we can grow will provide us with the 'riot' of colour that so many of us love to see. It is lucky, too, that the colours are more of the pastel persuasion than the flamboyant; tasteful gardeners like their riots restrained.

Four species, *PP. pulverulenta, aurantiaca, bulleyana*, and *helodoxa* will suffice to give us rose-red, orange, butter-yellow and creamy-yellow respectively. There is no hope at all that they will come true from seed, so what will emerge will be a subtly diverging range of hues in which the four 'primaries' will be found among light pinks and reds and every imaginable shade of yellow, cream and orange. Add

P.burmanica, in itself not very attractive, and you lend purples and mauves to the mixture.

These primulas will, if they are thoroughly well-suited, sow themselves. The trouble is that they will tend to do so in dense patches and it is best to lift these seedlings and plant them where they are really wanted. Some seed should be collected every year and sown under controlled conditions as well, especially from plants that have particularly good or appealing colours. They will not come true, of course, but you will be influencing selection towards your own tastes as the years go by.

Meconopsis—ideal companions for primulas in the moist, part-shaded places—are either perennial or may be monocarpic, which is to say that they die after flowering. The perennial species have a tendency towards monocarpism, but this can be averted if they are prevented from setting seed in their first year. It is advocated by some knowledgeable growers that they should be discouraged from flowering, and it is no doubt good advice; in my own experience it has been enough to cut off the flowering stems when the flowers have faded. *M.betonicifolia* (once known as *M.baileyi*) and *M.grandis* are the most reliable species in this respect and they thrive well in gardens where the summers are warm, although their colouring may show an intrusion of mauve into the pure blue in these conditions.

After their first year, every effort should be made to harvest and sow meconopsis seed. It is easily germinated, but damping-off disease strikes like a thief in the night and precautions must be taken.

The hardy geraniums, or cranesbills, can hardly be bettered as neighbours for the smaller shrubs and for growing generally in informal drifts in those parts of the garden that, so to speak, extend the character of the woodland plantings into the more open places. In really good, deep, well-cultivated soils, hostas will grow lushly in full sun, and are perfectly complemented by the more airy masses of the geraniums. Some geraniums will not set seed at all and have to be bought, but many do and they can soon be persuaded to make colonies just as large as you would like.

G.endressii comes from the Pyrenees and is, as you would expect, bone hardy. It is a plant of pleasing neatness and its prettily-divided, slightly grey, green leaves are perfect foils for its very long succession of candy-pink flowers. The form that is usually sold is 'Wargrave Pink', but I can see little difference between this and a great many of its seedlings as far as flowers go. The leaves differ, but not all that much. This is a plant that seeds itself very happily without making a take-over bid, but it is worth collecting some seed for controlled sowing elsewhere if it is wanted.

Geraniums are great artillerymen. The beak-like fusion of carpels unzips itself from the bottom when it is dried out enough, rather like a banana being peeled upside-down. Each zip has a bulbous end which, at the slightest touch, pings a fat, brown seed away into the distance. The record that I have observed is 36ft (12m)! The record cannot be officially ratified, as there was a very strong following wind but, nevertheless, great vigilance is required in collecting geranium seed.

In the informal settings in which the geraniums look so right, some of the cottage garden flowers come into their own. These were traditionally grown higgledy-piggledy among other plants and even intermingled with the vegetables and they never look better than when planted so as to appear as though they just happened.

Aquilegias are cottage-garden plants *par excellence* and they are among those which have been developed as seed strains. One of the best of these is the McKana Giant Hybrids, whose flowers are truly large, with great, dramatic spurs and colours that are quite magnificent. The stems are tall, too, so the blooms are held high and in proportion. A packet of seed will, all by itself, strike an old-world note in the most modern garden.

Campanulas, too, are summery, cottagey perennials that can be grown in among all sorts of other plants, including shrubs. Their tall spikes of blue or white are redolent of lazy, warm afternoons, the hum of bees, and the chink of tea-cups. That their flowers can be strutting their stuff only two years from seed is typical of herbaceous perennials; if you want to create moods or duplicate the slumbrous idylls of childhood, then a few packets of seed will do it.

Hollyhocks (*Althaea rosea*) are about as cottagey as you can get but they are not capable of being treated as perennials. Originally they were, but crossing with annual and biennial kinds, the incidence of rust fungus, and the inability of the roots to survive hard winters mean that they should be grown from seed every year. Seed from good plants, sown in mid-summer and overwintered in a cold frame, will flower in the following year. Some lucky folk in mild areas have very fine, single hollyhocks popping up all over their gardens each year with no encouragement whatever and very little rust. *C'est la vie.*

The informality of the cottage garden is just the place for alstroemerias. Once established, they can spread rapidly by their roots, so they have no place where each plant has its allotted station. One lady I know grows them for cutting for the house and has separate beds for them near her greenhouse. This is a good idea, as they benefit from being covered up in winter and she lives in the mountains.

The beautifully-marked flowers of alstroemerias, their rather exotic appearance, and their lasting qualities when cut make them deservedly popular perennials, but they are not by any means easy to establish. The ligtu hybrids are available as seed commercially, and most growers have more than enough to spare. The best way of dealing with them is to sow such seed in a pot of its own as soon as they are ripe. They should germinate quite soon and will then need to be looked after during the winter. The following year, the whole potful should be planted with about 3in (8cm) of soil above it, when the plants become dormant in late summer and with the greatest care being taken not to disturb the contents. Plant any shallower and mice will have the fleshy roots.

Alstroemerias may delay germination until the following spring. This is usually because the temperature has been too low after they have been sown. They require a warm spell, followed by chilling, and then another period of warmth for them to germinate.

Seed which is bought and which arrives in early spring may be dealt with by sowing it and then putting the pot or tray in heat—21°C is about right—for a month. Another month can then be spent in the refrigerator, before the sowing is returned to the warmth. The monthly intervals are not critical, and three weeks will do, but much longer will cause damage.

By far the majority of perennials (and just about all biennials) can be sown successfully in the late spring and early summer when there is plenty of atmospheric warmth and unheated cold frames can be used. Indeed, at this time, most of them will germinate perfectly well in an outdoor seed bed, made in the same way as one suitable for hardy annuals (see p.116–117).

The bed needs to be thoroughly watered—even soaked—because it can be a very dry time of year. The seeds are sown thinly in shallow drills and then lightly covered with soil. Woe betide the gardener who forgets at this stage to label each and every drill! The seedlings will be in place, with labels open to the depredations of birds, who pull them up and cats, who knock them over and then lie on them, until early autumn. Hefty labels are needed, and nothing beats foot-long (30cm) pieces of white-painted wood.

Transplanting is easy enough, but it pays to remember that winter is not far off with its winds and lifting frosts that tend to make plant and soil part company.

It would not be a good idea to sow fine seeds or those that are scarce or precious in outdoor seed beds. The frame is the place for these, where they can be protected and where they can be housed in their trays, sown with just the right depth of compost above them. Furthermore, the improvement in germination that comes from using peat-based composts applies just as much to perennials as it does to trees and shrubs, and you cannot make an outdoor bed with these. Fine seeds outdoors are almost bound to be over-covered and to become disturbed by rain-splash.

What is more and more likely as the gardener progresses is that he will abandon the outdoor sowing regime for the use of frames and a controlled environment. Once the easy perennials have been done once, they seldom need sowing again and can be kept going and increased by division. Activity on the perennial front grows to be increasingly involved with rarities and with plants whose antecedents are colder than those of the general run of perennial plants.

The next step is that he finds himself sowing his perennials along with his trees and shrubs in early spring, and may even resort to splitting batches of seed in half and sowing one lot in autumn. The lesson is really that the seeds of plants do not obey rules laid down for classes. They do not understand our calling them shrubs, trees, or perennials. All they know is the preservation of the species, and if a seed of a perennial has to behave like that of a tree in order that its species shall survive, then it is sure to do so.

A general, common sense guideline for sowing seeds of perennials is that the well-known ones, from which tendencies towards dormancy are likely to have been bred out, should be sown either outside or in a cold frame in late spring. Pure species, including anything new that comes along, should be either sown in autumn or given an opportunity to be chilled. As with any other group of seeds, maximum germination is only likely if additional treatments, beyond the scope of home gardeners, are given, but who needs it?

Alpines

The word 'alpines' is a much-misused one. Many garden centres have so-called 'alpine' departments, in which there is usually a long table bearing dried-up potfuls of dreary old rockery plants like mossy saxifrages, aubrietas, and snow-in-summer.

The true alpine gardener would not be seen dead near such displays, although you can sometimes pick up the odd unexpected treasure. He will patronize the specialist alpine plant nurseries and exchange plants with other members of his somewhat rarefied hobby, while his collection becomes ever more up-graded and ever more deeply interesting.

The real alpines—the plants of the high mountains, where snow blankets them in winter and where ice-spicules and grains of rock belabour them in the harsh winds of the short summer—are not easy things to grow. They are often temperamental and reluctant to become acclimatized to the cushy life of gardens at near-sea-level. They miss their snowy winter duvet, and they grow lush, fat, and unhealthy in the fleshpots of deep soils and calm air.

For all that, the world of the alpine gardener is probably more active and involved with the natural world than any other side of gardening. Every year sees several new additions to the flora of alpine gardens. Some may linger only for a season or two, but their beauty and their substance will have been enjoyed at first hand, even if ever so fleetingly. Quite ordinary people, sometimes either very young indeed or surprisingly old, venture into the most remote and dangerous places in search of new plants, or of those which have been with us once, never to be seen again.

In alpine gardening, as in other fields, the growing of plants from seed is increasing greatly, but it is among alpine gardeners that it is increasing the most. While ordinary rock-garden plants are still as loved as ever for their capacity for introducing the miniature, the fascination with new species knows no bounds. They must all—initially at least—be grown from seed.

The international exchange of plant material is extremely active among alpine gardeners. Because of the often very stringent phytosanitary regulations that governments impose on the movement between countries of vegetative plant material, seed is the only satisfactory means of exchange. This state of affairs applies to all other branches of horticulture as well, and it creates a strong imperative towards growing all kinds of plants from seed.

If you want to help a friend in a foreign country to grow a plant that is available to you but not to him, it is no good in the majority of cases to send him cuttings or small, rooted plants through the mails. There are ways of doing it that make it less likely that they will be discovered, but they are subtle, only known to a few, and illegal. The fact is that almost all plant material that enters, for example, the USA, is destroyed. Even with a phytosanitary certificate from the home authorities, it will be subjected to such sanitizing procedures that it will be most unlikely to recover.

Some countries will accept plants provided that all soil has been washed from the roots, but even then they may require the appropriate health certificate. Others demand that inspections shall have been carried out at intervals both of the grower's premises and plants and of any within a one-kilometre radius. What a hassle! It is, when all is said and done, simply far less complicated to put some seed in an envelope, address it, and consign it to the mails.

Even this is not yet legal, but with seed legality is easy to achieve. What you do is to obtain a small customs chit, write upon it 'flower seeds; no commercial value', stick the sticky label bit to your letter, and buy a stamp. Simple. The receiving customs may still open your letter to see if it contains cocaine or diamonds, but they will be careful and will not destroy your seed.

Of course, it is not just those plants that come to you from the wild or cultivation in foreign parts that you will want to grow from seed. As with shrubs and trees, there are alpines for whom seed is the method of choice for propagation. The cushion drabas and androsaces, for instance, are quite easily raised from seed, whereas they are the next thing to impossible from cuttings. I decline to say that they are quite impossible, as they can be rooted—just. Techniques developed to propagate the shockingly difficult genus *Dionysia* have revolutionized the taking of cuttings of minute, damp-prone shoots, but then *Dionysia* rarely if ever sets seed in cultivation and the extremely tricky process of vegetative propagation is made necessary. With the other high alpine cushion plants seed is set readily and germinates freely.

Most alpines that are grown from seed are species and have not had dormancy bred out of them like many border plants and annuals. They will to a large extent need periods of cold before they germinate in a warm spell. This will partly determine when you sow them, but things are not all that simple.

It will depend, for one thing, on when you receive the seed. Your own, home-saved seed gives you the choice of sowing in autumn or in spring, but distribution lists from societies, botanical gardens, and commercial sources usually arrive only in time to allow for sowing in the early spring or very late winter.

With trees and a good many shrubs, it is desirable to sow as many as possible of those that exhibit dormancy in the autumn, as their seeds may not store well and are more likely to be got at by predators if they are kept after failing to germinate in the first spring. Those that arrive late should, if possible, be encouraged to germinate in the first spring by giving them cold treatment in order to break their dormancy.

Alpines, on the other hand, are a bit of a problem if they germinate in the autumn or early winter, as their tiny seedlings are far too vulnerable to damp and to too long a period of risk from slugs and snails. Spring sowing involves chilling for many of them, but, unlike the sower of tree seeds, the alpine gardener is likely to sow a great many batches of seed, and the domestic refrigerator's capacity for seed—not to mention its owning family's capacity for patience—is limited.

A regime of sowing alpines in the very early spring in a place where they can be subjected to frost is really the one to be recommended. The exceptions to this are those seeds of known low viability, such as the Petiolaris section of *Primula* (they should be sown straight from the pod, even while still slightly green), and anything in Ranunculaceae, including *Pulsatilla, Ranunculus, Anemone*, and *Paraquilegia grandiflora* if you are lucky enough to get it.

Those that do not germinate from a spring sowing can then be kept for a year or even two, and there is a good chance of their coming up if the seed was good in the first place. Alpine seed does not attract mice in the same way that many tree seeds do, so you should not lose them while you are waiting for the happy event.

Seed sown in the first days of spring—mid-February in the northern cool temperate—will receive adequate chilling for a large number of species by mid-spring, provided that the trays or pots are not over-protected. A simple cold frame will do perfectly well and, even with its light firmly closed, it should allow a deep enough temperature drop.

The school of thought that advocates the sowing of alpines in autumn, after which they are to be left open to the weather, has a wide following, but not among those who grow the really top-echelon high alpines. It is quite all right for plants that are tough enough to stand becoming damp in winter, or simply just to tolerate life as minute seedlings in rough weather. For the aristocrats, however, it is risky, to say the least.

The in-frame, spring method does not demand, as the autumn, open one does, that each pot shall have at least one full inch (2.5cm) of chippings above the seed. This prevents disturbance to the seed and the compost by raindrops, and is supposed to discourage cats, without whom suburban gardening would lose much of its challenge. Raindrops and cats should not penetrate a well-made frame, and $\frac{1}{4}$–$\frac{1}{2}$in (6–12mm) of chippings will be enough to stop washing about caused by injudicious use of the watering can, as well as providing an initial degree of protection to the collars of the emerging and developing seedlings.

All kinds of weird and wonderful recipes are constantly being thought up for alpine seed-sowing. Precise mixtures, created with the assiduity of the practising alchemist, emerge, only to be discredited when they fail to germinate the philosophers' stone. Pots are depicted in drawings with layers of materials therein so arranged that their strata will—it is innocently believed—provide hors d'oeuvres, entrée, pudding, and cheese in order as the roots of the anthropomorphized seedling search more greedily downwards. 'Eat up your nice hoof and horn, and nanny will let you have some bonemeal.'

The trouble with deeply-involved hobby gardeners, of whom alpine buffs are the worst offenders in this respect, is that they cannot tell when to leave well alone. They are like revolutionaries who, having struggled against oppression for many decades, suddenly win and, unable to give up revolution, find new targets for their spleen.

The John Innes Institute found a perfect formula for composts after many years of experimentation. The best and most consistently successful growers of alpine plants have found that that Institute's seed mixture, mixed again with half its volume of sharp grit, provides a compost which it is just about impossible to better for raising alpines other than the true lime-haters and peat-lovers. It will do for germinating *Eritrichium nanum*, the most difficult dionysias, and the aretian androsaces. What more can the alchemists be seeking?

There is little doubt that, although plastic has taken the place of earthenware for plant pots throughout the horticultural world, there is a justified island of resistance among alpine people. Alpines simply do not like plastic pots, especially at the seedling stage. The addition of extra grit to the compost seems to have but little effect on the alleviation of their misery, but if plastic is all you can get, then it is something you will have to try. Far, far better is the clay half-pot, plunged to its rim in a mixture of peat and sand.

Your frame for raising alpines should, then, have a sufficient depth of this material in its bottom to allow pots of different depths to be plunged. It should, too, be constructed so that slugs and snails will not get in, as they will make a bee-line for the cool, moist niches between the pots and the plunge mixture. An excess of slug pellets encourages fungi, so do not overdo them, but lift each pot out occasionally and look for the beasts where they love to lurk — under the rims and the bottoms of the pots.

When it comes to giving clay pots of alpine seeds their initial watering, there is no substitute for standing them in a bath of water such that the water level is just below the soil level in the pots. This is at variance with what I have advocated for trees, shrubs, and so on, but there we are using peat-based composts with which this method does not work, and lightweight plastic trays which are liable to float before they can take up moisture.

The 'sweeping' method with the watering can works for alpines, but I still prefer the bath. I am not prepared to try to be more logical than that, as I recognize that I might just enjoy the soaking-from-below method, having practised it for so many years and having regarded seed-sowing as the first major act of each deliciously anticipated gardening year.

Alpines lend themselves less than anything other than bulbs to being grown as single specimens. There is something folorn and lonely about a solitary plant of *Pulsatilla vulgaris* that is not shared by a singular *Fatsia japonica*. Furthermore, a lot of small, individual specimens in a rock garden take on a spotty appearance with no sense of order or structure. They need, like heathers, to be grown in groups, or drifts, and there is no more economical or satisfactory way of doing this than by raising them from seed.

It is no good thinking in terms of drifts with plants like *Dionysia bryoides*, one well-grown specimen of which is about all that anyone can expect to raise unless he is approaching genius. Alpine seed-raising can provide you with the joy of growing the most utterly rare and beautiful plants in small numbers, over whose tiny details you will pore, spellbound, for hours. It can as well, though, provide you with a very pretty garden.

Bulbs

It is really very surprising that so few gardeners grow bulbs from seed. It hardly seems to cross their minds, and yet it is one of the most intriguing of all branches of seed-raising.

Of course, to many gardeners the word 'bulbs' conjures up large-flowered daffodils and things like the Darwin tulips, and these are easily and cheaply bought and give quick results for very little effort. So, too, do the Dutch crocuses and the English, Dutch, and Spanish irises. The trouble is that, although you can achieve a very colourful display by using the bulbs which are on the market, you are in fact growing a very restricted range of bulbous plants when you could be exploring what is a very large field indeed.

Many of the rarer bulbs are rare because they are difficult to grow, but a lot more are uncommon merely because they are small plants when compared with the highly-bred giants. Most of the bulbs that you will grow from seed will produce flowers that are quite small, but they will all be exquisitely shaped and natural-looking because they will be species for by far the most part. They will, too, be in proportion with their leaves, unless you elect to go in for *Colchicum*, whose members have no leaves at all at flowering time and massive, ugly ones when the flowers are long forgotten.

You will be able to savour the exquisite beauty of the tiny, early-flowering species *Narcissus* such as the white-flowered *N.watieri* from the Atlas mountains, the hoop-petticoat narcissi from North Africa and Spain, and the strange, autumn-blooming, green-flowered *N. viridiflorus* from the Middle East. The tiny, but gorgeous *Rhodohypoxis* will be yours in their hundreds, while any shady spot among your shrubs will sport its months-long succession of species of *Cyclamen*.

You will, quite soon, learn of the pleasure of making and operating a bulb frame, or of merely growing the more tender or delicate bulbs in your greenhouse. Some species require a period of 'baking' during the resting season, so their cultivation on pots or frames where they can be kept dry when required is essential, while others flower when our late winter weather is too much for them. A growing understanding of the conditions required by bulbous plants will lead you to want to provide them.

In short, you are highly likely to find that to embark upon growing bulbs from seed is to find a new world in gardening and a whole field of interest in which it is impossible not to become absorbed.

It is as well to sow bulb seeds as soon as they are ripe. There are exceptions to this—many lilies will germinate well from seed that has been stored in cool conditions over the winter, for example—but it is a very sound practice. Because you will be sowing species in the main, many of which will have originated in climates with cold winters, you will be up against dormancy problems causing long delays in germination if you do not sow the seed before dormancy develops.

When autumn comes, one's thoughts turn to seed-harvesting from shrubs and herbaceous perennials, and that is the season when most people sally forth with paper bags, scissors, and their short-sight spectacles. Even so, many shrubby seeds are missed because, like rhododendrons and their relatives, they refuse to conform and ripen their seeds in other seasons.

With bulbs, you have to adopt a year-round vigilance, as seeds tend to be ripening on some thing or another in almost every week of the year. Because you need to sow them as soon as they are ripe, you must also take on a year-round sowing regime which will only be broken by the really cold spells—and then you will be sowing your shrubs.

The ones from warm climates should be kept in the greenhouse to germinate—*Galtonia, Tigridia, Sparaxis* and *Watsonia* are among these—but the others can be given the same treatment as alpines (q.v.) as far as exposing them to cold is concerned. The schools of thought about covering the pots or not are as divided about bulbs as they are about alpines. Both bodies seem to get good results, but I prefer the closed, safer method.

There will probably be very little in the way of germination with the seeds from cold-winter plants until the following spring, and then you may have to wait a further year or two. What is certain, however, is that you will have far poorer and slower results if you keep all your seed until the spring and sow it then. Apart from the incidence of dormancy, many seeds will have lost their viability. I have never yet succeeded in germinating *Erythronium* when it has been stored, and *Crocus* seed can be killed rather easily, too.

John Innes seed compost with an extra dose of sharp grit of up to half its volume is recommended, as it is for alpine seeds. The very best grit is pure flint, milled to the size used to feed young chicks on poultry farms. For top-dressing, turkey grit, also flint, but much larger, is ideal. The thing with flint is that it is impermeable and holds no water, and is thus a perfect drainage material.

Again, as with alpines, it is best to use clay pots if at all possible and to plunge them in a peat and sand plunge medium. On the whole bulbs are not as sensitive to plastic pots as alpines are, but clays are better, especially for those bulbs from places with hot summers.

Bulb seed should be sown thinly because the seedlings must be left in their pots for at least one, and up to three years. It is not a good idea to turn them out of their pots until young bulbs have formed, and this usually takes at least a year. When it takes longer, the young plants should be fed, preferably with a liquid feed.

With very small young bulbs it is best to pot them on, but larger ones can be pricked out and planted in the garden in the autumn. Very rare plants, of which you may only have just a few in one pot, are safest if the whole potful is removed from its pot and planted in a bulb frame.

Wherever you plant them, however, do take care with those that, as mature bulbs, will need a summer baking. In their youth they cannot take it in the same way and are likely to dry up too much and to shrivel. How this squares with their behaviour in the wild is something I do not know, but it is so, anyhow.

Some bulbous plants grow very rapidly from seed to flowering. Many lilies will flower the year after sowing, while some will do so the same year, as will tigridias. Most take from three to five years, with some tulips taking even longer if they have gone dormant before germinating. I once had *Tulipa sprengeri* in flower a tedious seven years from my having received the seed, and *T.tarda* has taken six on two occasions.

Perhaps it is the prospect of such a long wait that has put many people off growing bulbs from seed. It should not, as it is commonplace with shrubs for that sort of period to elapse before flowers are seen. Indeed, some of the greatest treasures of the plant world are very long jobs indeed. *Magnolia campbellii*, sown from the earliest introduction of 1865, first flowered in Ireland in 1885, and not for another ten years in England. That it was worth the wait is beyond doubt, and it makes people who think that four years or so is too long an interval to make bulb seed worth thinking about look mighty impatient.

Vegetables

There seems at first glance to be no point at all in growing vegetables at home. In most cases it is cheaper in the long run to buy them at a store, where they will be available all nice and squeaky clean and wrapped up ready for the cook.

There are arguments in its favour, but they are not all that strong. One says that an amateur grower does not have to cost his time when working out the economics of home-growing, while another states that vegetables straight from the garden have more flavour than store-bought ones.

In truth, the amateur should cost his time. Time which is spent on activities that are unprofitable, either in the economic sense or in the sense of spiritual profit, is time which could be spent elsewhere. It is very difficult nowadays to justify vegetable growing economically, and the relaxation and satisfaction that it engenders can well be obtained from other activities, including gardening ones of different sorts. Those for whom vegetable-growing is a chore might try working out just how much it is costing them. They would soon give it up. The flavour argument has a lot in its favour. So many people say that fresh garden vegetables remind them of the way things tasted in their youth that there must be something to it. It is impossible to be sure, as taste is such a subjective thing, but it is true that vegetables lose some of their flavour between the market garden and the store shelf.

Nevertheless, the difference is, I believe, quite small compared to what it could be and is not enough to justify an uneconomic activity. What would make home vegetable growing a profitable proposition in the spiritual, if not the economical sense, would be to increase the flavour differential greatly. If at the same time the aesthetics of vegetable growing could be made more gripping, a lot would have been achieved.

Total justification comes when varieties are grown that are not available commercially and have either greatly increased flavour over store-bought vegetables or are prettier, either in the garden or on the table. Some, too, may have no equivalent in the stores and therefore need no justification as long as they are culinarily worthwhile.

This is well-illustrated by the so-called French salad potatoes. Potatoes are, of course, grown from seed tubers and not from seeds at all, but the point that they exemplify applies to other vegetables as well.

This group of potatoes consists of several varieties of small, waxy-fleshed tubers of the most incredibly intense flavour. It is almost as if the essence of the potato taste had

111

been refined into concentrated form and liberally injected into them. 'Kipfler', 'Pink Fir Apple' and 'Etoile du Nord' are the best for most purposes, but the amazing 'Bleu Maroc' has no peer as a salad-only potato of truly heroic flavour.

This variety—translated sometimes to 'Morocco Blue'—has flesh that is of a true purple and the tubers are very small and rounded. Boiled, and then sliced and served cold, it is a gastronomic experience beyond belief. Its extraordinary colour is a fine addition to the range of salads or of *hors d'oeuvre*, but I would not serve it sauté.

The only variety that is available today is 'Pink Fir Apple', and that is very scarce indeed. Seed of the others, including 'Bleu Maroc' appears to have disappeared. This is very sad, as amateurs who grew vegetables for the right reasons might have given them a heyday instead of persisting in growing varieties with big yields and only a small margin of flavour over the store potatoes.

How long will the Brussels sprout 'Rubine' be grown. Rather like the blue potato, is it to be condemned because of its buttons which are dark red instead of green? It is indeed a pretty sight in its rows, with its red foliage, and its flavour is far superior to any other variety—so much so that one might hope that it would find favour in America, where the sprout is not highly regarded. Is it that vegetable growers are so stodgily entrenched in their habits and outlook that means that the out-of-the-ordinary is to be mistrusted?

Let us, on the contrary, put aside our blinkers and use our vegetable gardens for excitement and fun, while they enrich our tables with new tastes or better versions of old ones. Let us not dismiss beetroot 'Burpees Golden' because it is yellow, instead of red. Rather let us approach it as an item in its own right and appreciate its wonderful flavour without wearing a think bubble in which 'beetroot' and 'red' are forever linked.

We will then be fully prepared for 'Purple Cape', a cauliflower which would be a disaster commercially. Instead of the pure white heads so beloved by the buying public, this has deep purple ones. The flavour is nothing short of superb, especially when the vegetable is served raw in crudités or even with the cocktails. Cooked, it turns green, but retains the high-class taste.

A quite wide acceptance of yellow tomatoes in recent years is an encouraging sign, and varieties such as 'Yellow Perfection' and 'Golden Sunrise' are universally available. They have rich, satisfying, fruity flavours without the acidity of many of the market forms. 'Gardeners Delight' is red, and is exceptional in the deliciousness of its sweet, nonacidic flavour, although its fruits are too small for it to become popular with the commercial growers, who persist with the dreadful 'Moneymaker', perhaps the most tasteless tomato of all time, and an exemplar of exactly what we are talking about.

Once the commercial market latches on to something worthwhile, it is time for the amateur to stop growing it and to find something else upon which to spend his time and with which to fill the available space. There is not much point now in growing *mange tout* peas when every supermarket stocks them in perfect condition for eating and with very little, if any, loss of flavour. Some few years ago they were unheard of outside the gardens of those who had discovered how tasty they were, but now they are everywhere, and it is no bad thing.

The same does not yet apply to calabrese, but it soon will. This is a sort of green version of purple-sprouting broccoli which has the advantage of being ready only three months after sowing. This means that successional sowings will give a crop from early summer until the hard frosts, whereas the purple plant takes nine months to cutting from seed and has a short season of productivity. The taste of calabrese is just as good as that of purple-sprouting broccoli—perhaps even better in a nutty sort of way—and it is a much better payer of the rent for its land.

Kohl rabi is in an intermediate stage. It is still a vegetable that is associated with amateur growers but has recently found its way on to the shelves here and there. It is a strange, but quite neatly attractive plant with a white, swollen stem just at and above soil level. It is a nice, nutty flavour and can be eaten raw as well as cooked.

Swollen roots, rather than stems, are the parts of jicama that are eaten. In the United States this is reaching the stores and becoming popular after a dalliance with amateurs on its way from Mexico. It is related to the broad bean, but seed formation is discouraged in order to concentrate the plant's energy into its root system. It is best sown in a greenhouse and then planted out in a sunny place, where it can develop its turnip-like root, whose flavour is a great delicacy when it is sliced and eaten raw with a little lemon juice and salt. In Chinese cookery they retain their flavour when diced and very quickly stir-fried.

The Chinese cuisine is reckoned to be one of the two of the world's greatest—the other being the French. There are, in fact, several regional cuisines which are quite as distinct as those of Germany and Greece, for example. Nevertheless, the vegetables that are used are fairly universal and are well worth growing by households who have learned that it is a barbaric practice to serve green vegetables unless they are just slightly undercooked.

Chinese cabbage (pe tsai) is a delicious salad vegetable when eaten raw after being chopped, and it is very good when stir-fried. If the idea of fried cabbage turns you off, do not be dismayed; stir-frying is not by any means the same as frying, and the cabbage emerges crisp, tasty, and not remotely greasy. We have it stir-fried with oyster sauce at home and the fact that it tastes of meat rather than of oysters goes to show how one should not prejudge Chinese cookery.

There are several varieties of Chinese cabbage available as seed and it will grow wherever other brassicas will. 'Market Pride' is an early variety, producing large, tight, round heads, while 'Che Foo' is another heading variety which is later. Chinese leaves are non-heading Chinese cabbage; the round-leaved and the serrated forms of 'Santo' are both good.

Chinese chives are like the pig—everything can be eaten except the squeak. The bulbs and leaves are edible, and so are the flowers, whose scent is more like that of roses than of members of the onion family. The plant can be used for flavouring, like garlic, or stir-fried as a vegetable. It can also be used in European dishes as onions.

Bunching onions are asiatic onions that look like mini-leeks and are extremely succulent, including the leaves. One or two varieties can be obtained as seed and are well worth it.

Aubergines are used in Oriental cookery quite a lot and are being grown in western gardens much more recently than hitherto. They are expensive to buy and constitute an economic crop, as one or two plants in a greenhouse are all you will need to satisfy the wants of most families for this occasional vegetable. The egg plant is attractive in some eyes (but not in mine) and is a good bet until prices come down. It can be grown successfully in the open if there is plenty of sun in a warmish climate.

Asparagus is most definitely a good economic proposition. It is profitable in the aesthetic sense, too, as it is one of the most dearly-loved ingredients of flower arrangements. It is expensive to buy and is regarded still as something of a rare delicacy, while most gardeners think of it as difficult to grow and then only from bought-in roots.

In fact, the best way of growing asparagus is to give it plenty of manure, but not to go to great lengths in making a traditional asparagus bed. If it is grown from seed sown every year, you can establish a four-year cycle so that you always have plenty of shoots to pick. The first year, it is sown and germinated and planted out to about 2ft (60cm) apart, and the second season sees it allowed to gain strength while being weeded and top-dressed with more manure. The third year can see a little cutting only, but in the fourth the crop can be used to the full before being dug up and discarded in favour of the second-year sowing which will be ready in the fifth year—and so on.

After that first glance, a deeper look at the possibilities of sowing a better vegetable garden provides you with the chance of broadening your gardening horizons once again through the medium of seed. An open mind, unfettered by the ho, hum, here we go again stultification that tradition has inflicted, will soon find the delights of American land cress, a plant that tastes like water cress but needs no water, or of the highly nutritious and flavoursome celtuce. Perhaps you, too, will base your salads on endive and pass on to others the mysteries of couve tronchuda, okra, and scorzonera.

Annuals

An annual is a plant that, by its very nature, germinates, flowers, sets seed and dies all in one year.

As a botanical definition that should be crystal clear, but it will not do to explain the use of the term 'annual' in gardening. Accurate definitions in horticulture are as rare as hens' teeth, and at the moment there isn't one for annuals. This is because what we grow as annuals include tender perennials as well as genuine botanical annuals.

For our purposes, then, we can do much better by defining an annual as a plant that germinates, flowers, sets seed and dies all in one year *in a given environment*. For instance, species of *Impatiens* are perennial, although short-lived in nature. In cultivation they are treated as half-hardy annuals.

The terms 'hardy' and 'half-hardy' are themselves rather odd and have no real basis in logic. What we may take them to mean is that plants are either hardy at the germination stage or not—after that the weather is going to be warm until they die, so designations of hardiness become irrelevant. There is a third class—tender annuals—but these are outside our brief, as they have to live under glass all summer. Examples of tender annuals are *Primula malacoides*, *Calceolaria* hybrids, gloxinias, and *Streptocarpus*.

Hardy annuals can pass their entire existence from germination to death in the garden and need no artificial aids. Sunny areas in well-drained soils should be chosen, and sowing should be delayed if the soil is sticky from rain. The ideal is to sow in a soil that has previously been well-watered and which has dried just enough to render it friable.

The reason for this is that if the soil is too dry, it will take such a heavy watering to wet it sufficiently that air will be driven out and a hard, cake-like surface will be formed which will prevent the entry of air or further water. If it is too wet, the physical actions involved in sowing will create a paste-like environment for the seeds which will be even worse.

The site should be well and truly cleaned of all weeds and other rubbish, especially perennial weeds, large stones, and the bones that constitute the dog's life savings. Then, when the soil is pretty dry, it should be raked and then gone over inch by inch by the gardener, using his feet as compressors. He will adopt a gait not unlike that known to the medical profession as *locomotor ataxia*; the weight on the heels while a short, rapid shuffle is engaged in with the feet almost touching. It is tedious for the gardener but immensely enjoyable for the spectators, especially if they are about ten years old and possessed of sharp wits. 'Garn, lightnin'. Gerrit in the net then,' was the contribution of one budding master of repartee.

Raking again will produce a firm bed with what is called a 'fine tilth'—an extraordinarily archaic expression with overtones of meticulous peasantry—into which shallow drills can be made without any trouble. Of course, those who have clay soils whose best use is in making pots will never achieve this. Their best tilth will be such that the largest lumps will be the size of golf balls and the smallest would dwarf *petit pois*. They must try, however. Life is not a bowl of cherries.

Two oz per square yd—or 60g per square m if you prefer—of a general fertilizer will keep the wolf from the door if applied at this stage. The difference between good hardy annuals and really bad ones usually begins at the seed-bed stage, so it is worth taking every trouble and giving the plants every assistance.

As the seeds are to be sown where the plants are to grow, drills should be drawn with that in mind and not in uniformly straight lines as you might when sowing perennials in their seed bed. As an alternative to watering the whole site, which involves a delay while you wait for it to become friable again, you can water the bottoms of the drills and then cover with dry soil after sowing. Broadcasting the seeds on the site is practised by many gardeners, but the results can be disappointing because it is difficult to see them when raking afterwards and you cannot tell how deep the seeds are or even where they are.

The time to be doing all this will vary from year to year because of the weather, but the equinox should be past by up to two months but no longer.

As with perennials, a great many hardy annuals can be sown under glass and in a little heat quite a lot earlier, and this is certainly worthwhile with some of those that are hardy in the true sense of the word. Sweet peas, for instance, can be got under way much earlier, after their hard coats have been chipped, and the odd ones that are hard to germinate because of dormancy problems need to be dealt with earlier as well.

Molucella laevis, bells of Ireland, needs chilling to break its dormancy. Two to three weeks at 1—5°C in the 'fridge, followed by being brought into real warmth—say 21°C, should do the trick after a further month or so. This is a good plant for floral arrangers, who tend to despair of it because they try to germinate it like other hardy annuals. Serves them right for liking green flowers.

Half-hardy annuals will fail if an attempt is made to germinate them and grow them on in their early stages in the open. They need to be sown under glass and can be started as early as the new year, although most things will be better off rather later than that because it is easier to maintain a consistent atmosphere when the worst of the winter cold is over. Nevertheless, they are sown in advance of the hardy annuals, with the possible exception of marigolds, which can (just) be treated as hardy annuals and sown outside with them.

Sowing them is just the same as anything else—a peat-based compost in trays with bottom heat. Thin sowing goes without saying, or should do by now, and fine seed can, like any other, be mixed with dry sand and sown with it. Once again, the finest seed should not be covered, and this is especially important with begonias which also require a high degree of humidity.

Many gardeners find *Impatiens* (busy lizzie) seed very difficult to germinate. The genus is, in fact, one with a positive lust for germination, as anyone will know whose garden has been invaded by Himalayan balsam, but the desirable ones have a need which is not all that easy to provide.

They require constant humidity of a very high order, and they are so sensitive to it that if one part of the seed is in a less humid environment than another, germination will not take place. What is more, the seeds are very light-sensitive and need to be sown on top of the compost. The paradox that ensues is one in which light is provided only at the expense of humidity around the exposed part of the seed coat.

My friend and BBC colleague, Geoff Hamilton, has solved this problem with dramatic results, and he has done it at a perfectly timed moment for such research, as the varieties of *Impatiens* that are becoming available to amateur gardeners are greatly increasing.

He draws very shallow channels, or drills, in the surface of the compost and then sows lightly in them. The channels are then filled with a fine grade of vermiculite. This material holds a vast amount of water in relation to its weight and, by being in contact with the seeds, keeps the humidity constant all around them. The beauty of the method is that light can penetrate to the seeds in sufficient quantity to allow germination to take place.

It goes without saying, of course that the pots or trays should be wrapped in film or kept in a propagator at the maximum possible humidity until germination has taken place. Temperature should be a constant 21°C.

Those plants that everybody calls geraniums but which are really pelargoniums need more than the 18–21°C that other half-hardy annuals require. These are the bright red

'Paul Crampel' types, the ivy-leaved geraniums and the others in that easily-recognizable but appallingly badly-named group. The seeds are very expensive indeed—monumentally so in some cases—so there is no point in trying them unless you are prepared to take the trouble to see that they can germinate in temperatures of near to 24°C.

These temperatures are not easy to attain without the expenditure of a great deal of costly energy, so the best way of coping is to sow the seeds on edge and place the pots in the airing cupboard on the floor. If you live in one of those countries with unvented water systems you will not have such a thing, but I am sure that you get the picture and can devise something similar. This will not work with seeds that need light for germination, so I should keep it for the geraniums and the cucumbers. Try, too, to learn the art of peace negotiation, as this is the second major piece of domestic machinery that you will have taken over.

Above all, keep an eye on seeds set to germinate in dark heat, no matter how it is achieved. If you forget them, they will come up and produce long, blanched seedlings that are immediately useless.

Half-hardy annuals are usually sown quite thickly and then pricked out into other trays, either singly or, as with lobelia, in small clumps. This saves space where you want germination to take place, as the transplanted seedlings can take temperatures 10°F lower or less. Slow, gentle hardening-off is the secret of success in growing-on, and the greenhouse temperature can be lowered gradually before the outside air is allowed eventually to take over.

Annuals are thought by many people to be easy and time-saving. Nothing could be further from the truth. They are, quite simply, extremely labour-intensive and the easiest thing in gardening is to grow annuals badly.

They make a great deal of growth in just one season, and during that time they produce a great many flowers. All this takes a lot of food and a very large amount of water, so it follows that they need constant attention in terms of watering and feeding if they are to be any good at all.

Sun is their friend and shade their enemy, and they are not too keen on wind, either. You may well find yourself doing as much staking of annuals as you would if you had one of those herbaceous borders that everyone says are so hard to manage without an army of helpers.

What is worse about annuals is that they are ... annual. One season is all you get and then they are gone. You have great bare patches of soil all winter which will only be filled when you have gone through the whole tedious process again. To be forced to garden like this, year in, year out, would be my idea of purgatory. Not Hell—it would, at least, still be gardening.

However, there are times when it is a blessing to be able to have some instant colour. A new garden looks pretty uninspiring while the young plants are all spaced out looking lonely, and some colourful annuals will make it look very jolly for a year or two. Some of my friends who are professional gardeners like annuals very much and one, who lives and works in Florida, says that they comprise his favourite side of horticulture. It is noticeable that while I am to be found gaping at the bromeliads growing on tree-branches and being bowled over by cycads and winter-flowering hibiscus, he is gazing adoringly at the beds of annuals and bedding pansies. So, if you must grow annuals, I am not to gainsay you but must shoulder the burden of duty and point you in the direction of the best ones.

The Fleuroselect awards are given to annuals which have been sent for trial at a series of testing stations all over Europe and increasingly in other parts of the world. Varieties that win awards will, therefore, be amenable to growing well in a wide variety of conditions and climates, as well as being of outstanding ornamental quality.

The standard of impartiality, fairness, and judging skill is extremely high among the Fleuroselect panels. While seed comes from commercial sources and is judged within the trade, the organization is such that it is impossible for favour to be applied to any variety other than that which it earns as a plant or flower in its own right.

Good seed catalogues mark items with the Fleuroselect symbol if they have gained awards, and you may have the utmost confidence in these. I may not personally like *Calendula* Fiesta Gitana (which you may find rendered as Gipsy Fiesta), but I cannot but recommend it if calendulas are to your taste. Similarly the new bedding dahlia Sunny Yellow is one which should be looked upon with favour.

Sunny Yellow is an F1 hybrid, and this is another factor that makes an annual rather above the run of the mill. Without going into the genetics of plants, which would be extremely boring even if I knew anything about them, F1 hybrids combine uniformity with hybrid vigour. They are usually hand-pollinated, which costs money, so they tend to be rather more expensive than open-pollinated seed, but they are worth it, even if you get fewer seeds in the packet.

An award from a national horticultural society is always a major cachet for a plant or for a seed strain. If your seed catalogue mentions items which have won such awards or have received Fleuroselect awards, or which are F1 hybrids, or any combination of the three, then your garden will be the richer for them as, I am truly sure, mine would be too.

Deciduous azaleas are worth growing from seed, not least because the resulting plants are often as good as expensive, named varieties.

Seed types **1** *Incarvillea delavayi*, **2** *Lunaria rediviva*, **3** *Malva moschata 'Alba'*, **4** *Centaurea macrocephala*, **5** *Allium giganteum*, **6** *Astrantia major*, **7** *Argemone grandiflora*, **8** *Salvia patens*, **9** *Meconopsis betonicifolia*, **10** *Ligularia sibirica*

Seedlings of *Echinacea* 'Robert Bloom', such as this one, should be labelled as *Echinacea purpurea*, but are mostly much better than the species.

Meconopsis grandis hybridizes readily with *M. betonicifolia* and most plants seen are of this hybrid, *M × sheldonii*. Nevertheless, they are almost always magnificent.

A fortuitous combination of *Allium giganteum* and *Centaurea macrocephala*, both of which are readily raised from seed.

A eucalyptus seedling at the correct age and height for planting. It is only five months since the seed was sown.

It would be very hard to grow too many plants of *Lilium regale*. Grown from seed they are inexpensive and can be planted in large numbers.

Ornamental cabbages and kales are fashionable bedding plants in France and the United States. Sown just as for the vegetable garden, they seldom reach the kitchen.

The Names of Plants

The more a gardener involves himself with growing plants from seed, the more he will need to be competent in handling plant names in botanical Latin.

This is because most of the things he will meet are species, and it is impossible to separate a species from its scientific name. What is more, he is going to be seeking to grow plants from seeds that have come from parts of the Earth where his mother tongue's rule does not run or where, even if it does, it has different meanings.

If I write to a friend in the United States of America, asking for some seeds of wake robin to be sent to me in England, I will eventually receive *Trillium grandiflorum*. A request from America that I should send seeds from England of wake robin would elicit material from *Arum maculatum*. That I would get by far the better deal is, of course, irrelevant; what really matters is that the use of vernacular plant names can cause great confusion, even occasionally within the same country.

Lovers of native wildflowers are very fond of using what they perceive to be the traditional names. This is admirable, but is a pursuit that should be undertaken with caution. For one thing, a plant may be known in one part of the country by one name, and by quite another elsewhere. For another, there may be so many names used for a plant that any one may mean very little to a great many people.

For example, Jack-go-to-bed-at-noon is more commonly known as Goat's Beard, but by no means everywhere. In some parts of England, to which it is native, 'Goat's Beard' would bring forth nothing but blank looks, while in Australia it would mean something entirely different anyway. If *Tragopogon pratensis* had been the name used instead, there could have been no confusion at all. Again, *Arum maculatum* has over a dozen vernacular names in English, and several more in the languages of continental Europe. It might be argued that the male/female allusions in 'Lords and Ladies', 'Stallions and Mares' fall into a recognizable group, but who but the most eruditely eclectic plantsperson is going to know what 'Aaronstab' is?

Where the ardent seed-raiser is different from his fellows is in the inevitability of his one day finding himself the custodian of horticultural treasures that can truly be beyond price. Seed received, say, from a botanical party who have obtained once-in-a-lifetime permission to visit a restricted area in a remote and difficult part of the world, and probably of a species long lost to cultivation, is of immense value. If the recipient boasts that he cannot put up with 'all those long Latin names', then he is unlikely to preserve the name of the species through all the batches of seed trays, pots, and pottings-on that will be required, let alone keeping it accurate when passing plants on to others.

To tell the truth, Latin names are not really all that long. The longest that I can find is *Echinofossulocactus*, and even that is by no means as lengthy as Welcome-home-husband-though-never-so-drunk. Neither are they as daunting to the person of reasonable education and wit as such people make out. It is, surely, an affectation that leads them to trot out such tongue-stoppers as antirrhinum because it is, they think, an 'English' word, while eschewing *Hedera* for its Latinity.

The first part of a plant's name (e.g. *Hedera*) is its generic name—the name of the genus to which it belongs. While it would be unwise to press the analogy too closely, it is, in some respects, the 'surname' of the plant. It is always spelt with a capital initial letter and written in print in italic letters. Many botanists and gardeners write it underlined in their correspondence in order to indicate italic letters—I must confess that I do not. I am far too lazy and think, anyway, that my correspondents do not need me to tell them when something is in Latin.

Italics are also used for the second component, the species epithet. The generic *name* and the species *epithet* together make up the *name* of the species (were we to feel the onrush of a real wave of pedantry we would refer to the 'specific' epithet, but there are limits). This is a sort of forename which singles out just the one species from among the others in the genus, as in *Hedera colchica*.

Quite often batches of seed will be received from plant hunters which have only a generic name and, usually, a collector's number (see p. 49). An example might be *Viburnum* sp. VdL 950. This means that, at the time of collection, Mr. Van de Laar did not know to which species of *Viburnum* the plant belonged from which he collected seed. This does not reflect on the gentleman's plant knowledge; indeed, were the rest of us to aspire to his erudition, we should find ourselves with a long row to hoe. It is to say that the plant did not fit any of the species of *Viburnum* as we knew them at that time.

Later, the plant will be classified into a species, either one which already exists, on there being good grounds for its inclusion, or into an entirely new one because the plant is new to science. Our viburnum might (only it is unlikely, because it is a fictional one) turn out to be such a new species and, because it is covered with little spines, be called *V. spinuliferum*. It is the duty, no less, of the raisers of its seedlings to pay the utmost attention to the persistently accurate spelling of its name from the moment it becomes known.

There are many examples of plants that have gone into very wide circulation with wrong names because of carelessness on the part of those who originally raised them from seed. Great confusion takes over and usually lasts, not for a year or two, but for decades.

One such was a little, pink-flowered epilobium which was sold in the trade and found in a great many gardens as *Epilobium kai-koense*. Nobody seemed to know where it came from or even of which continent it was a native, although many believed it to hail from China, Japan, or somewhere like that.

The mystery was solved after many years when it was found to be a form of *Epilobium glabellum*, a white-flowered species from New Zealand. The pink one had been discovered growing in the Kaikoura Mountains of the South Island, and should have been called *Epilobium glabellum* var. *kaikourense*. Whoever failed to preserve the name was guilty of an insufficient realization of and respect for the importance of Latin names.

Even worse was the case of a tiny poppy with a very odd name. Variously labelled, catalogued, and sold as *Papaver totewokii*, *P. tokwokii* and *P. tatwaki* among other sobriquets, this charming, yellow-flowered plant was hardy, but rather short-lived. Once again, the raiser of the original seed had boobed in a big way. Where on earth did the plant come from? What was its provenance? How could we find it in the wild again to see if there were white forms—or red ones?

It might as well have come from the planet Krypton, had it not been for the person who discerned amidst all the 'toks' and 'woks' the name of the distinguished Japanese botanist Tatewaki. Tatewaki-san was a botanical authority whose knowledge of a small field was so great that he was asked to place plants within certain genera into species. Anything possibly new to science would be reviewed by him and if necessary, placed in a new species. The name of that species would carry his name in full or as an abbreviation after it in Roman letters.

Gardeners do not normally label their plants with the author's name or abbreviation, but academic botanists do. Thus, *Hedera colchica*—generic name plus specific epithet—is written in botanical circles as *Hedera colchica* (K.Koch) K.Koch. This is because Herr Koch first called it *Hedera helix* var. *colchica* and later revised his own work.

Our poor little poppy, it turned out, had been called after another Japanese botanist, Miyabe. Miyabe-san was to be honoured by Tatewaki by his naming the poppy species for him, and his, Tatewaki's name would stand as that of the author. The correct name for the plant was *Papaver miyabeanum* Tatew, where Tatew is the usual abbreviation for Tatewaki. That such a pretty plant should acquire a grotesque parody of its real name was a result of great irresponsibility made even greater by the lack of due honour to Miyabe and Tatewaki.

In discussing these examples, we have used another kind of name, in which a third Latin component arrives. Latin names are constructed under the binomial system, originally refined and standardized by Linnaeus and now accepted internationally. It is the two-name system which we have already applied to *Hedera colchica*. Trinomials—three Latin words in a row—are forbidden by the International Code of Botanical Nomenclature, so how do we further subdivide?

Where a species has, in the wild, a variation which is too great to allow of its being ignored but not great enough to warrant consideration of species status in its own right, it may be designated a variety. This is not the same as a variety which arises or is bred for in cultivation and which should be referred to as a cultivar. A variety is designated by the abbreviation var. in Roman letters, as in the now superseded *Hedera helix* var. *colchica* of Herr Koch.

The botanical world is coming round to preferring the designation 'forma', abbreviated to f., as an additional way of avoiding confusion, and, one presumes, because it is itself a Latin word. The fastigiate version of the English oak thus becomes *Quercus robur* f. *fastigiata*. There seems to be little consistency about 'var.' and 'forma' just yet, so do not worry about it—just avoid mixing up wild forms in Latin with cultivated ones in a vernacular language.

If you raise a new plant, you can up to a point, call it what you like, but there are rules that must be obeyed if your name is to obtain acceptance.

Let us say that, after many years and hundreds of batches of seed, you have raised a new spectacularly superior rhododendron. Its parenthood is known, but each parent is an unnamed hybrid of immensely mixed blood. You decide, naturally with the kindest motives—nothing whatever to do with fiscal or testamental considerations—to call it after your Aunt Fiona.

You may call it *Rhododendron* 'Fiona', provided that there is no other of that name already, and provided that you have the good sense to provide a description or plant material or both to the Royal Horticultural Society, who are the Registration Authority for *Rhododendron* internationally. The name is written in Roman letters and always takes single inverted commas.

You may not call it *Rhododendron fionae*, because it is not a species, and you may not call it *Rhododendron* 'Fionae', because all cultivar names must be in a vernacular language and not in Latin or a Latin form. Any vernacular language will do, and it is permissible to translate. 'Blaulicht', for example, may be rendered as 'Blue Light'.

It is not the thing to call it *R.* 'Aunt Fiona', because styles and titles are not permitted. Nobody could now call a rose 'Parkdirector Riggers', thank heaven. Neither, of course, may her testatory favours be seduced by calling your rhododendron 'Mrs. Money-Baggs'. However, 'Fiona Money-Baggs' is perfectly all right.

It is very easy to understand how people can be put off using Latin names for plants. Scientists keep telling us that names we have used all our lives must now be changed, and harmless names like *Cornus canadensis* pass away in favour of such monstrosities as *Chamaepericlymenum canadense*. There are, we are told, good reasons for this and even cases in which names that should have been changed are 'conserved', such as *Pittosporum* Solander, which is preferred to *Tobira* Adans, in order to avoid confusion, even though the rules say that it should not be.

Whatever our opinion may be, we as gardeners are unqualified to judge the merits or otherwise of plant name changes. As raisers of seed we have a duty to name the resultant plants as accurately as we can, and if that means using a name that goes against the grain but is the right one, then so be it.

To be put off by the pronunciation of Latin is to make a fundamental mistake of scholarship. Only the ignorant will feel smug about using botanical Latin as they were taught to use Classical Latin. The two are as different as grape juice and brandy. Botanical Latin is not a dead language but a living, international one, and it has developed over the many centuries during which Classical and Church Latin became fossilized. There are words like *corolla* that mean nothing like their original meaning, and other words that have been coined purely within the botanical language. It has been pronounced in many ways and still is, although the two accepted variations, the Reformed Academic and Traditional English, are used by most people. It boils down to whether you say Yulius Kighsar or Julius Seezer.

I confess to using bits of each, combined with one or two inconsistent idiosyncrasies. It does not worry me, but I am almost fanatical about getting the spelling right on labels. What you say and what you write down are there to be understood, and they are the means by which your individual contribution to the endlessly fascinating and valuable world of seed-raising can be handed on.

Woody Plant List

In the following list, one hundred and thirty genera are dealt with. In some cases, where only one or two species are in cultivation, the instructions or suggestions are specific to them; in the majority of cases, however, there is not room to mention all the species. Indeed, a very large tome indeed would have been necessary in order to do so.

Most genera are reasonably subject to generalization. The oaks, for example, constituting as they do a very large genus indeed, can conveniently and accurately be broken down into just two divisions for the purpose of examining their germination requirements. The considerably larger genus *Rhododendron* is even more obliging; just one sowing regime covers the lot.

Of course, gardening being what it is and gardeners being a group of widely experienced people with deeply enquiring minds, somebody will find that they have found the odd species that behaves quite differently from what is set out here. This is inevitable. Perhaps they will be mollified by the fact that almost all the information given derives from first-hand experience, and it will be noted that some of my more notable and consistent failures are catalogued here.

Much of the material that involves suggestions for achieving germination will be seen as less than the ideal by those who have professional experience. Gardeners are neither foresters nor nurserymen in the main, and neither of these sets of professionals needs any advice from me. Professionals though, seek to maximize their germinations, and there are several instances in which a more complicated method of dormancy-breaking would produce much better results.

The general idea is that the gardener is unlikely to require all that many plants of a woody subject. Sometimes a simple method will produce just a few seedlings, while such regimes as the alternation of warm and cold periods of stratification would result in many more. It is not felt that the amateur gardener has either the time or the inclination to go to the lengths that the professional must in order to do his job properly.

The term 'stratification' does not, in fact, appear in the list. I have deliberately kept things simple by speaking of 'cold treatment', particularly as the alternation of warm and cold is hardly ever mentioned. It is, nowadays, rather an outmoded word in this context, as we no longer place our seeds in strata between layers of sand or peat. The refrigerator has changed the world dramatically as far as seed-raisers are concerned.

Lest domestic strife should break out like an epidemic, let it be said that that member of the household who goes in for seed-raising to the extent that the refrigerator is destined to be taken over for some weeks during the winter and early spring, should first ask permission to use a very small amount of space in the family machine. From then onwards, a gradual invasion by degrees of the places where the bacon and butter should go can be tried up to whatever limits of toleration ensue.

The emphasis throughout on the use of bottom heat may well cause some controversy, especially among those who have never used it and who have nevertheless achieved good results. The fact is that I have found, in common with many others, that it is a great boon and can be shown statistically to have a significant—and sometimes dramatic—effect on germination rates.

Climatic differences should be taken into account. Where seeds exhibit dormancy that is broken by a period of cold, they will be more likely to get it from an autumn sowing in an unheated structure in a colder climate. Those of us who garden in mild places will have greater recourse to spring sowing and the refrigerator. It should never be forgotten, though, that freezing *per se* is of no benefit; it is that band of temperatures just above freezing where the anomalous expansion of water occurs that does the job. Chilling is the operative term. Even this is no good unless the seeds can imbibe water, and a moist, but not saturated medium is essential.

Above all, if the gardener who has been consistently successful with methods which are different from those which I suggest then changes them, this whole book will have been in vain, as its whole ethos is one of asking the reader to think and to experiment. If you have already done so and it works, please carry on in the same way and let your fellow plant-lovers know what you have done. The body of horticultural knowledge is not so complete that it can do without the wisdom that resides in the minds of the many thousands of gardeners too modest to impart it.

Plant name	Description	Common name	Flowers	Hardiness and general comments	Germination
Abies species	Evergreen, coniferous trees	Silver firs			Germination rate is low because of high proportion of unformed seed. Most species benefit from cold treatment in moist peat for twenty-eight days at 1.5°C, but small quantities of seed may be sown untreated in early spring after the embryos have been dissected out.
Abutilon vitifolium	Evergreen, large shrub or small tree		Mauve or blue, early summer	Slightly tender	Sow in early spring with bottom heat.
Acacia species	Evergreen, small trees	'Wattles'. *A dealbata* is 'Mimosa' of florists	Early spring or summer, according to species	Tender	Pour boiling water on to seeds and allow to soak for twenty-four hours, then sow immediately. Gently free cotyledons from seed coats if necessary when seedlings are growing.
Acer species	Deciduous shrubs or small trees	Maples			Viability of most maples is low and they are vulnerable to drying. Sow in autumn, except for spring-ripened seed, which should be sown on collection. *Acer griseum* is very difficult, but some success has been obtained by sowing dissected-out embryos.
Aesculus species	Deciduous, tall trees	Horse chestnut; Buckeye			Vulnerable to drying. Sow on collection; germination in spring. Cotyledons do not appear above soil.
Ailanthus altissima	Deciduous, tall tree	Tree of Heaven			Give cold treatment for two months at 1.5°C or a little higher in moist peat.
Albizia julibrissin	Deciduous, small tree		Pink, summer	Mimosa-like. Tolerates much more frost than generally supposed	Treat as for *Acacia* or chip the seed coats.
Alnus species	Deciduous, medium trees	Alders			Sow in early spring.

Amelanchier lamarckii	Snowy Mespilus	White, spring, before leaves	Foliage coloured in spring and autumn. Lime-free soil	Differential dormancy allows small germination of spring-sown, untreated seed. Cold treatment by sowing in pots in unheated frame in autumn will give better results.
Aralia species	Angelica trees	White, early autumn	Very expensive in nurseries, so species best from seed	Low germination rate due to proportion of unfilled seed. Cold treatment for thirty days at 1.5°C, followed by warming and further chilling for three weeks.
Arbutus species	Strawberry trees	White, late autumn at same time as fruits		Soak fruits in water to soften them and then remove the seeds from the pulp and dry. Drying the fruit is difficult, as moulds often intrude. Sow immediately in unheated frame or sow in spring after cold treatment for one month at 1.5°C.
Aronia species	Chokeberries	White, spring	Conspicuous red or black fruits. Bright autumn colour	Remove seed from fruits, whether fresh from the garden or dried from the seedsman. Cold treatment for two months at 1.5°C gives adequate germination. Alternating cold and warm is optimum treatment but not necessary for amateur requirements of plants.
Azalea — see *Rhododendron*				
Azara serrata		Orange, scented, mid-summer	Fairly tender	Extract seed from white berries (formed in hot summers) and sow in bottom heat in early spring.
Berberis species	Barberries			Berberis are easy from seed if it is sown in the autumn. Either whole berries or individual seeds may be sown. Spring-sown seed gives much-reduced germination.
Betula species	Birches			Sow in early spring under *light* shading and do not cover seed. Light necessary for germination.
Broussonetia papyrifera	Paper mulberry		Grown for extraordinary, varying lobing of leaves. Orange fruits on female. Rare in gardens. Hardy	When seed can be obtained, sow in early spring with bottom heat. Plant out at least three to obtain berries.

Plant name	Description	Common name	Flowers	Hardiness and general comments	Germination
Buddleia species	Mostly deciduous, shrubs				Easy from spring-sown seed. *B. davidii* can become a weed; best to buy varieties. *B. colvilei* has large, deep rose flowers and is eminently desirable. It germinates abundantly but is a bit tender.
Callicarpa bodinieri var giraldii	Smallish shrub		Late summer	Unique metallic mauve colouring of flowers and berries	Germination varies from year to year. Sometimes adequate from early spring sowing, sometimes a failure. Cold treatment in moist peat of extracted berries can give good results but can also fail. Said to need several specimens for berries, but the author does not find this to be so.
Callistemon species	Small, evergreen shrubs but medium in warm climates	Bottlebrushes	Red or yellow, summer	Much hardier than generally thought, especially if sheltered from wind	Very easy from spring-sown seed; bottom heat an advantage. Treat against damping-off.
Carpenteria californica	Evergreen, medium shrub	Tree anemone	Large, white, summer	Hardy, but best against a sunny wall	Very easy from spring-sown seed. High germination rate.
Carpinus species	Deciduous, medium trees	Hornbeams			Harvest seed while still slightly green and sow immediately in unheated cold frame. Germination the following spring.
Carya species	Deciduous, medium trees	Hickories			Outside the USA, imported American nuts must be used. Cold treatment, either in moist peat or on their own in a plastic bag, for two months at 1.5°C. If nuts are received direct from cold storage, sow at once.
Catalpa bignonioides	Deciduous medium tree	Indian Bean tree	White, purple markings, late summer		Sow in early spring. Easy.
Ceanothus species	Small to medium shrubs, evergreen or deciduous	Californian lilacs	Mostly blue, spring or summer		*Ceanothus* species do not readily set seed outside the USA, but seed is sometimes offered for sale in Europe. Germination is quite good if the seeds are soaked in boiling water and left in the cooling water for twenty-four hours.

Species	Description	Common name	Flower	Notes	Germination
Cedrus species	Large trees. *C. brevifolia* is a small tree. Conifers, evergreen	Cedars			Germination is easy in the spring. Cones may be stored unopened until the spring, when they will open in hot water. Storage of naked seed is unwise, as the seeds are oily and soon deteriorate.
Celtis species	Deciduous, medium trees	Hackberries, Nettle trees			Germination from spring-sown seed with bottom heat is adequate.
Chamaecyparis species	Evergreen conifers, medium to large	False Cypresses			Poor germination rates due to unfilled seed. Cones open if dried in the sun and release seeds. Differing dormancies within batches means seedlings appear in flushes or a few at a time in successive years.
Chamaerops humilis	Evergreen, small palm			The only European palm. Makes thickets, only 2ft (60cm) tall. Hardy in mild areas	Sowing in spring with bottom heat gives small germination. Warm treatment—in moist peat at 21–24°C gives improvement, but germination should be watched out for during the treatment. Fourteen days should see some signs of germination.
Chimonanthus praecox	Deciduous, medium shrub	Wintersweet	Pale yellow, purple centres, winter, scented.		Seed is sometimes offered. Sow as soon as obtained. *Chimonanthus yunnanensis* is still very rare.
Clianthus puniceus	Evergreen climber	Lobster claw, Parrot Beak	Large clusters of bright red, or white in *C. p.* 'Albus', spring	Rather tender	Easy from seed sown in bottom heat in early spring.
Colletia species	Evergreen, medium shrubs, foliage mainly spines		Pink or white, scented, early autumn	Very spiny and highly decorative	Occasionally sets abundant seed which must be caught as it drops, as the plants are too spiny to handle. Germinates prolifically if sown in bottom heat in early spring.
Cordyline australis	Evergreen, small tree	New Zealand Cabbage Palm	Panicles of white in summer, scented	Hardy in mild areas	Not to be confused with the Cabbage Palm, *Sabal palmetto*, the State tree of Florida. This is a member of the Lily family and not a true palm at all. Seeds germinate well in spring but need bottom heat.

Plant name	Description	Common name	Flowers	Hardiness and general comments	Germination
Cotoneaster species	Evergreen or deciduous, from small trees down to prostrate shrubs				Such a common genus should be easy from seed but is not so. Many are doubly dormant because of hard coats and internal dormancy. Seed, removed from the berries, may be rubbed between sheets of sandpaper to scarify the seed coats, and then given alternating hot and cold treatment in moist peat.
Crataegus species	Medium shrubs and small trees	Hawthorns		Many very fine and ornamental plants with all-year appeal	Germination is difficult and good results are rare. Best method for gardeners is to sow immediately when ripe, having extracted the seed from the berries. Place the pots in an unheated frame but early enough for thorough warming to take place. Subsequently allow a winter's chilling. Seedlings should appear in mid-spring, but some species may take a further year.
Cupressus species	Medium to large conifers	Cypresses		Most species are not hardy in cold climates	Treat seed with a fungicide powder. Cold treatment for one month at 1.5°C.
Cytisus species	Shrubs	Brooms			Soak seeds of all species in boiling water and allow to cool for twenty-four hours. *C. battandieri*, the pineapple broom, does not need this and germinates well if sown in bottom heat in spring.
Daphne species	Small shrubs			Highly ornamental shrubs with great fragrance when in flower	Remove seed from the berries while they are slightly unripe and sow immediately. This is usually in mid-summer. Alternatively, give cold treatment in moist peat for three months at 1.5°C. Daphne seed should not be dry-stored, as it will lose viability and germination will be poor. Net berries of *D. mezereum* against birds.
Davidia involucrata	Deciduous, small to medium tree	Handkerchief tree, Ghost tree, Dove tree	White bracts, spring	Staggeringly beautiful when in flower	The fruit has a dry flesh, within which is a hard, ribbed nut. This contains from three to five seeds. Many failures occur through sowing the nut whole. It should be split and the seeds extracted and sown immediately. Nutcrackers may be used with care!

Species	Common name	Description	Flower	Feature	Notes
Dipelta floribunda		Medium shrub	Pink, spring	Very lovely in flower, like a superior weigela	This shrub is very rare in gardens. One of the reasons is that it is not easy from cuttings; the other is that it produces masses of seeds which totally refuse to germinate. It is, therefore, mentioned merely as a warning.
Embothrium coccineum	Chilean Fire bush	Small tree or large shrub	Flame red, late spring		Semi-evergreen plants, remarkably beautiful. Seed germinates well with bottom heat in spring but plants sometimes refuse to grow on. *E. c. lanceolatum* is the best source.
Enkianthus campanulatus		Deciduous, small to medium shrub	Sulphur-bronze, spring	Magnificent autumn colour. Lime-free soil	Sow on lime-free compost in early spring. Do not cover seeds.
Eucalyptus species	Gums	Evergreen, small shrubs to large trees			Sow with bottom heat on the surface of the compost in early spring. Do not cover except for the larger seeds of the tropical species. Seeds are black among red-orange unfertilized ovules. Contrary to the advice of many authorities, the author has found that adequate germination has been obtained *without exception* in over seventy species, including several for whom the need for special treatment has been claimed.
Eucryphia lucida		Evergreen, medium shrub	White, late summer	Slightly tender	The only species of which the author has first-hand experience from seed. This was sown with bottom heat in early spring and germinated quite well.
Euonymus species		Medium to large shrubs, deciduous or evergreen			Seed is best sown in autumn, as it stores badly. This will also break dormancy and give good germination in spring.
Fagus species	Beeches	Deciduous, large trees			Beech nuts (mast) should be sown immediately in an unheated cold frame. They will not tolerate becoming dry. Imported seed arriving late should be cold-treated for one month at 1.5°C.
Fatsia japonica		Medium evergreen shrub	Heads of white in autumn	Large, palmate, shiny leaves. Perfectly hardy in sheltered places	Remove seed from fruits and sow with bottom heat in spring. Fair germination.

Plant name	Description	Common name	Flowers	Hardiness and general comments	Germination
Fraxinus species	Deciduous, tall trees	Ashes			It is to all intents and purposes essential to sow ashes immediately upon collection. Sown in pots in a cold frame, germination may take place over two or three years.
Fremontodendron californicum	Evergreen, medium shrub		Large, golden yellow all summer	Needs a sunny wall	This is easy from seed but the seedlings will be inferior to the variety 'California Glory', so sowing is not recommended.
Gaultheria species	Evergreen, small shrubs		Spring or early summer	Excellent plants for peat walls etc. Must have lime-free soil	Cold treatment is desirable but, in general, adequate germinations will result from spring sowing.
Genista species	Small to medium shrubs, some small trees	Brooms			Despite being leguminous plants, whose seeds usually have hard seed-coats that hinder germination, *Genista* species mostly germinate quite well from spring-sown seed. Bottom heat is an advantage. The Mount Etna Broom, *G. aethnensis* germinates freely in this way.
Ginkgo biloba	Tall tree	Maidenhair tree		Lovely, golden autumn colour. Unique foliage and habit	Seed is not set until trees approach fifty years old. Seed is enclosed in a foul-smelling fruit which must be allowed to rot and then can be washed from the nuts. Not worth it. Imported seed should be soaked in boiling water and allowed to cool for twenty-four hours before sowing in spring, preferably with bottom heat.
Gleditsia species	Small trees	Locusts		Attractive foliage. Some species flower well, but the flowers are insignificant	Boiling water treatment in spring.
Grevillea species	Small shrubs		Crimson or yellow, long-flowering	Slightly tender. Non-limy soils	Germination from spring-sown seed is good. Bottom heat helps. *G. rosmarinifolia* and *G. sulphurea* are hardier than generally thought.

			Flowers	Features	Notes
Gymnocladus dioicus	Deciduous, medium, slow-growing tree	Kentucky Coffee tree		Leaves pinkish when young, golden in autumn. Twigs silvery in winter	Soak seeds in boiling water and allow to cool for twenty-four hours before sowing in spring.
Hakea species	Evergreen, medium shrubs		White in hardy species, spring	Remarkable foliage, rather conifer-like	*H. sericea* and *H. microcarpa* are hardy in all but the coldest gardens. Easy from seed sown in spring, preferably with bottom heat.
Hebe species	Small to medium evergreen shrubs			Mostly require protection in severe winters	Easy from spring-sown seed, especially with bottom heat. *H. salicifolia*, with white flowers, is perhaps the hardiest and is given to self-sowing when happy.
Hippophae rhamnoides	Deciduous, medium shrub	Sea Buckthorn		Silver leaves. Orange berries on female plants. Excellent seaside windbreak	Remove seeds from berries. Give cold treatment for three months at 1.5°C or a little higher, then sow in spring.
Hoheria species	Medium trees	Ribbonbark	White, late summer	Rather tender	Easy from spring-sown seed with bottom heat
Hydrangea species	medium shrubs; one or two are quite large				Seed is easily missed once it is ripe. Collect by putting heads upside-down in paper bags. Seed minute, *do not oversow*. Easy if sown in spring. Bottom heat not essential.
Hypericum species	Small shrubs		Bright yellow		Easy from spring-sown seed.
Idesia polycarpa	Deciduous, medium tree		Large panicles, green-cream. Not on young trees	Large, noble foliage, red leaf stalks. Red berries on female trees	Abundant germination from spring sowings. Plant three for berries if you have room, or just one specimen for the beautiful foliage.
Ilex species	Evergreen shrubs or trees	Hollies			Dormancy of holly seed is very profound and is compounded by hard seed-coats. Extract seeds from berries and sow in pots in a cold frame. Forget about them and allow yourself to be surprised when seedlings appear a few at a time over three years or even more.

Plant name	Description	Common name	Flowers	Hardiness and general comments	Germination
Juniperus	Evergreen conifers of varying sizes	Junipers			Junipers are difficult to germinate. The best thing to do is to remove the seeds from the berries, sow them, put them in a cold frame and hope. Odd seedlings will occur from time to time.
Koelreuteria paniculata	Deciduous, small tree	Golden Rain tree	Yellow flowers, late summer	Yellow autumn colour	Spring-sown, untreated seed will germinate, but very poorly. Scarification by rubbing between sheets of sandpaper increases germination dramatically
Kolkwitzia amabilis	Deciduous, small bush	Beauty bush	Pink, early summer		Some germination from untreated, spring-sown seed with bottom heat. Cold treatment for thirty days at 1.5°C appears to give better results.
Laburnum species	Deciduous, medium shrubs		Yellow, spring		The seeds are poisonous, as is the rest of the plant. Germination is good if the seed is scarified between sheets of sandpaper or individually chipped.
Laurus nobilis	Medium to large evergreen shrub	Culinary Bay	Cream, spring	Leaves used in cooking	Remove flesh from seeds and sow in autumn if possible. Otherwise soak in warm water (not boiling) and allow to stand for twenty-four hours before sowing.
Leptospermum species	Evergreen, medium shrubs	Tea Trees	White, pink or red, summer		Good germination from spring sowing with bottom heat.
Leycesteria formosa	Deciduous, medium shrub		White, wine-red bracts, summer	Attractive shrub with green stems	Extract from berries and sow in spring.
Liriodendron tulipifera	Large deciduous tree	Tulip tree	Tulip-shaped, lime-green. Not on young trees	A noble tree with distinctive foliage, turning butter-yellow in autumn	Ideally this should be sown in autumn. Spring-sown seed should be given cold treatment for about six weeks at 1.5°C.

Species	Habit	Common name	Flower	Notes	Germination
Lonicera species	Small to medium deciduous shrubs	Shrubby Honeysuckles			Spring-sown seed gives an adequate germination in some species. Others need cold treatment, while still others may require alternating warm and cold. Probably the best idea is to sow all shrubby honeysuckles in the spring and expect delayed germination, a few at a time.
Lupinus arboreus	Smallish evergreen shrub. Not long-lived	Tree Lupin	Yellow or purplish, all summer		The easiest woody plant from seed by a distance. Sow in the spring. Germination in a very few days.
Maclura pomifera	Deciduous, large shrub or small tree	Osage Orange		A hardy plant. Grown as an impenetrable hedge and for its orange fruit	Said to be slightly dormant, but spring sowings, after soaking in cold water for twenty-four hours, have produced good results.
Magnolia species	Medium to large trees. Mostly deciduous, but some evergreen spp.				Seed pods are like large, lumpy sausages. They turn red or dull red when the seeds are ripe and then split. Each seed then hangs by a mucous thread. Seeds are enclosed in a red or bright orange pulp. Lay out to dry in the sun and the seeds will be freed from the pulp. Sow immediately in individual pots in a cold frame. Bought seed, arriving late, may be given cold treatment for thirty days at 1.5°C, but storage can reduce the viability of the oily seeds.
Malus species	Deciduous, small trees	Crab apples	White, pink, or dark red, spring	Some of the best small garden trees	Spring germination is very difficult. Crab apples should be sown in the autumn in pots in a cold frame for the best results.
Melaleuca species	Evergreen, small shrubs		Bottlebrush-like, purple, red, or yellow	Rather tender	Germinate easily in spring with bottom heat.
Melianthus major	Medium sub-shrub			Grown for the magnificent, grey-green, pinnate foliage. Rather tender	Spring sowing with bottom heat is best, although germination rates may be affected by the presence of unfilled seed.

Plant name	Common name	Description	Flowers	Hardiness and general comments	Germination
Menziesia species		Small shrubs	Cream, pink, or purple, spring	Peat-loving plants. No lime	Sow in spring in the surface of a peaty compost and do not cover.
Myrtus species	Myrtles	Small to large shrubs	White, summer	Mostly rather tender	Extract seeds from fresh or dried berries and sow in spring with bottom heat.
Nerium oleander	Oleander	Small shrub	Pink, midsummer to autumn	Tender	Although the author has propagated oleanders from cuttings, he has never succeeded with seed, although he has tried several methods several times. Never having had the chance, he has not sown fresh seed immediately when ripe—the best bet?
Nothofagus species	Southern beeches	Medium to large evergreen and deciduous trees		*N. procera* and *N. obliqua* are hardy, large trees. *N. antarctica* is a hardy medium tree. Many other spp. will stand severe frost	Sow in autumn in cold frames.
Olearia species	Daisy bushes	Small to medium shrubs	Mostly white, a couple of purple-flowered species		Sow in spring with bottom heat. Failure is usually due to unfilled seed set in cultivation.
Oxydendrum arboreum	Sorrel Tree	Deciduous, large shrub or small tree	White, late summer	Brilliant red and yellow autumn colour. No lime	Treatment as for rhododendron q. v.
Paeonia species	Tree-peonies	Medium shrubs	Red or yellow, spring	Fine, bold foliage	*PP. delavayi, potaninii* and *lutea* var *ludlowii* are quite common in cultivation and seed is easily obtainable. Doubly dormant. Sowing in spring will result in production of the root; a further period of cold, followed by warm will induce shoot production. Either leave for a year or give the second period of cold artificially.

Species	Type	Common name	Flower	Notes	Propagation
Paulownia species	Deciduous, medium trees	Foxglove trees	Heliotrope. *P. fortunei* has white flowers, spring	Large, tropical-looking foliage. Flowers well after mild winters	Very easy from spring-sown seed, especially with bottom heat. Very prone to damping-off, but this is easily controlled with copper compounds. Do not cover seed; light is essential.
Penstemon species (shrubby)	Dwarf shrubs		Various, mostly pink or red, spring		Shrubby penstemons are usually propagated by cuttings. Viable seed is sometimes set and it germinates well if sown in late winter in an unheated frame. 'Well' in this case means anything above forty per cent.
Perovskia atriplicifolia	Deciduous, small shrub		Lavender-blue, summer	Grey foliage	Germinates readily in spring with bottom heat.
Phellodendron amurense	Deciduous, medium tree	Amur Cork tree	Greenish white, beloved by bees	Corky bark, attractive, aromatic pinnate leaves	Seed that has been stored properly (i. e. kept cool) will germinate readily if spring sown with bottom heat. Imported seed is sometimes not of good quality, but a few seedlings usually result. Most gardeners will be content with this.
Phlomis species	Small shrubs	*P. fruticosa* is 'Jerusalem Sage'	Yellow or lilac-pink (*P. cashmeriana*)		Easy from spring-sown seed. Bottom heat is an advantage.
Phormium species	Technically, evergreen perennials	New Zealand Flax	Dull red, summer	Architectural plants of great quality. Included here in line with most catalogues	After years of trying to raise plants from home-saved seed, the author is of the opinion that seed introduced from New Zealand is the only hope. This is only mentioned in order to spare others from disappointment.
Photinia species	Deciduous or evergreen, medium shrubs	*P. arbutifolia* is the Christmasberry	White, spring. Evergreen spp. need warm climate for flowers	Evergreen spp. grown for foliage and coppery new growths	Imported seed germinates readily when spring sown.
Phygelius species	Small shrubs, partly deciduous	Cape Fuchsia	Pink to scarlet, all summer	The yellow forms do not come true from seed	Easy from spring sowing, especially with bottom heat. Seed is often set in warmer gardens.

Plant name	Description	Common name	Flowers	Hardiness and general comments	Germination
Phoenix canariensis	Medium palm	Canary Islands palm		Tender	Sow in spring in a temperature of 24°C. Thrives in mild parts of the cool temperate.
Phyllodoce species	Evergreen, dwarf shrubs		White, purple, blue or pink, spring to early summer	Peat-loving and lime-hating	Treat as for *Rhododendron*, q. v.
Pieris species	Evergreen, medium shrubs		White, spring	New growths bronze or reddish. Lime haters.	Treat as for *Rhododendron*, q. v.
Picea species	Evergreen, medium to large conifers	Spruces			Spruces can be sown in spring in an unheated frame. Germination is good if the seed has not been stored for too long.
Pinus species	Small to very large evergreen conifers	Pines			Sow in late autumn or early winter for germination the following spring. Place in an unheated cold frame. It is important not to sow too early in the autumn, as pine seedlings do not take kindly to frost. Sown in spring, dormancy will have built up and cold treatment will become necessary.
Piptanthus laburnifolius	Large shrub, partly evergreen	'Evergreen Laburnum'	Yellow, May	May require protection of a wall in very cold places. Deciduous in cold winters	Rubbing between sheets of sandpaper, or chipping the seedcoats assists germination, but results are surprisingly good with no treatment at all.
Pittosporum species	Evergreen, medium to large shrubs. Rarely of tree size		Mostly purple, *P. tobira* has cream flowers, scented		Sow the sticky seeds as soon as they are ripe. Place in heat in early spring.
Platanus species	Deciduous, large trees	Planes			Sow in spring. Germination will be good in an unheated frame.

Name	Common name	Description	Flowers	Hardiness / Fruit	Propagation notes
Populus species	Poplars	Large trees			Poplars are difficult. The difficulty is not in initiating germination; that is quite easy as long as the seeds are not covered—they require light. It is the absolute necessity of maintaining an even degree of moisture that makes the raising of poplar seed a job that is beyond most amateurs who cannot keep a constant watch. Over wetting is fatal, but any degree of drying is, too, especially at the stage where the seed coat has been raised above the compost and has not yet been shed.
Protea species		Small to medium evergreen shrubs	Several colours	Tender	There is a growing interest in trying these magnificent, South African shrubs out of doors in mild gardens. Germination is difficult, but *P. cynaroides* and *P. barbigera* have proved to be relatively easy when sown in early spring with bottom heat at a temperature of around 21°C and with high humidity. This regime will suit most of them, but germination rates are low and seeds are rather expensive.
Prunus species		A large genus of plants, from small shrubs to medium-sized trees			*Prunus* seeds have stony coats which, surprisingly, are not a barrier to germination. Almonds germinate better when the stone is cracked open, but in general it is embryo dormancy that has to be overcome. This can be done by cold treatment in damp peat for ten weeks or so at the rather surprisingly high temperature of 2–4°C, but it is suggested that seed should be sown in an unheated frame in the autumn.
Punica granatum	Pomegranate	Deciduous, large shrub	Large, red, summer	Tender, but stands a series of hard frosts if sheltered from wind. Needs sun and heat for fruits	Germinates well in spring with bottom heat.
Pyracantha species	Firethorn	Evergreen, medium shrubs	White, summer	Orange, yellow, or red berries lasting all winter	Remove from the berries and sow straight away in an unheated frame.

Plant name	Description	Common name	Flowers	Hardiness and general comments	Germination
Quercus species	Medium shrubs to mighty trees	Oaks			Oaks are divided into the white oaks, e. g. *Q. robur*, *Q. bicolor*, and the black oaks, e.g. *Q. rubra*, *Q. coccinea*. All oaks should be sown immediately they are collected, although despatch by air will be quick enough if they are sown as soon as they arrive. White oaks will begin to germinate straight away, but black oaks will wait until the following spring, as they have embryo dormancy which is absent in the white oaks. Such vernacular names as 'Red Oak', 'Scarlet Oak', do not have anything to do with the black and white divisions. Black oaks will dry out fatally if sowing is delayed until the spring, so there is no point in trying treatments used for other seeds with embryo dormancy.
Rhododendron	Dwarf to large shrubs; some trees. Majority are evergreen, but some (inc. Series Azalea) are deciduous				Rhododendrons should be sown in spring where they do not receive frost. A temperature of around 7°C is ideal, and this can be provided in a frost-free greenhouse. Cold-frame sowings should be delayed until all but light ground frosts are over; rhododendrons are therefore best sown after most other trees and shrubs. Sow on the surface of a peat-based compost and allow plenty of light but no direct sunshine. Do *not* sow in autumn, as the seedlings are too small to survive without constant attention. Prick out when large enough to handle without injury either to the upper parts of the plants or to the tiny root systems.
Rhus species	Deciduous, large shrubs	Sumachs		Notable for brilliant autumn colour	Soak seed in very hot water and allow to continue to soak while cooling for twenty-four hours. Sow in spring.
Ribes species	Deciduous, small to medium shrubs	Flowering currants		Spring, some spp very decorative	Sow in autumn in an unheated cold frame. Seed coat and embryo dormant.
Robinia species	Deciduous, small trees	False Acacias	Pink or white, early summer		Soak in boiling water and allow to cool for twenty-four hours. Sow in spring.

Species	Growth habit	Common name	Flowers	Germination notes
Rosa species	Small to medium shrubs; climbers			Roses germinate best when the seeds are extracted from the hips as soon as they have turned red. Further delay may result in drying which will delay or reduce germination. Dormancy is caused by the seedcoats and autumn sowing is best so as to allow substances in the seed coats to leach away naturally. Pots or trays may be brought into heat in the spring with advantage.
Rubus species	Rambling and climbing shrubs	Ornamental Brambles		Put the berries in a food blender in water to separate the seeds from the pulp and sow in the autumn in an unheated cold frame. Germination may be delayed for one or two years from the following spring.
Salix species	Small to medium deciduous trees	Willows		Willow seed is extremely vulnerable to becoming even slightly dry. It should be collected as soon as the capsules start to turn yellow, and should be sown without delay. Germination is extremely rapid and may occur in as little as one or two days.
Salvia species	Deciduous, small to medium shrubs	Sages	Many colours, mostly red or blue shades, summer to winter	Of the seventy or more species currently in cultivation, nearly all are beautiful. Many but by no means all are tender. All have aromatic foliage. All species germinate readily in spring, but bottom heat is a definite advantage.
Sambucus species	Deciduous, medium shrubs or trees	Elders		Elder seeds have hard seedcoats and embryo dormancy. They may be sown in autumn, but germination may be delayed for eighteen months or more. Alternatively, the seed can be soaked in water for twenty-four hours and then given cold treatment for three months at 1.5°C. The best media are sand or vermiculite.
Sophora species	Small to medium deciduous trees	*S. japonica* is 'Japanese Pagoda Tree', *S. tetraptera* is 'Kowhai'	Very beautiful trees with conspicuous white or yellow flowers in spring or summer	Scarification or chipping of the seedcoats, or soaking in hot water are recommended by various authorities before spring sowing. The author's experiments with *S. tetraptera*, received fresh from New Zealand, gave no better results than with control batches sown with no preparation whatever. Germination was uniformly high under all conditions.

Plant name	Description	Common name	Flowers	Hardiness and general comments	Germination
Sorbus species	Small trees	Mountain Ashes, Whitebeams, etc			The best results are obtained from sowing as soon as the seeds can be removed from the ripe berries. Red berries should be gathered before birds take them. Spring sowings should follow ten weeks of cold treatment at temperatures only just above freezing, using moist sand or peat. Without treatment, spring sowings may wait one or two years before germinating.
Spiraea species	Small to medium shrubs				Spring sowing in an unheated frame will suffice for just about all the species.
Symphoricarpos species	Deciduous, small shrubs	Snowberries			Too difficult. Not worth it.
Styrax species	Deciduous small trees	Snowbells	White, summer		Difficult but worth every effort. Soak in water for three days and then give cold treatment at 1.5°C for six weeks. Alternatively, sow in an unheated frame in autumn.
Syringa species	Deciduous, medium shrubs	Lilacs			Lilac seed does benefit from either cold treatment or from being sown in the autumn, but the advantage gained is so slight that spring sowing is recommended, with or without bottom heat.
Tamarix species	Deciduous, large shrubs	Tamarisk	Pink, spring, summer or autumn	The best seaside windbreak	Sow fresh seed in autumn and stand back!
Telopea truncata	Deciduous, smallish shrub	Tasmanian Waratah	Crimson, summer	Lime-free soil	Beware unfilled seed. Good seed germinates quite well in spring with bottom heat.
Taxus species	Evergreen, small trees, conifers	Yew			Very slow germination. Although varying degrees of cold treatment work quite well, there is little gain over autumn sowing, as seedlings may not appear for a year or two anyway. Complicated systems of warming and chilling are used, but who among us has the time?

Thuja species	Evergreen, large conifers	Arbor Vitae			Dormancy is occasionally encountered, but thujas should germinate well from spring-sown seed, particularly *T. plicata*.
Trachycarpus fortunei	Evergreen palm	Chusan palm	Creamy yellow, summer	Perfectly hardy, but easily damaged by high winds	Sow in spring in a temperature of 24°C.
Vaccinium species	Evergreen, small shrubs	Blueberries, Bilberries, Cranberries, etc		Lime haters	Remove seeds from berries which have become very dark and show a bloom. Dry well before storing. Sow in unheated frames in spring. Germination may be very rapid for part of the sowing, further seedlings may emerge over the next two years.
Viburnum species	Small to medium evergreen or deciduous shrubs				This is a very large genus, so it is not possible to give hard and fast guidance for sowing. Most species, however, exhibit double dormancy, so the best plan is to sow in early spring and then leave the pots for a year or so where the weather can get at them but in shade and protected from vermin. Either extracted seed or whole dried berries may be sown.
Yucca species	Woody members of the Lily family, medium-sized		White, summer		Yuccas germinate well from spring sowings. Bottom heat helps. Soaking in water for twenty-four hours may well improve germination rates, as the seeds are somewhat hard-coated.

Perennial List

In the following list a minimum of detail is given because the genera are for the most part well-known. There is little point in drawing distinctions where none really exist; neither is it practicable to set out such things as flower-colour and season, when almost all the plants flower in the summer or late spring, and each genus may well have members whose blooms cover a wide spectrum of colours.

The plants listed are those with which some degree of difficulty may be encountered in attempts to raise them from seed. By far the greater majority of perennials are quite easy, but there are a few that present problems.

The list states the nature of the problem in each case, and suggests a method of overcoming it which has, in the author's experience, given satisfactory results. While some perennials will germinate in as little as a week, most take about a month. Problem seeds can take a year or more, so it is unwise to throw pots out precipitately. A tray of wild-collected seed of *Iris innominata*, which germinated ten months after sowing, and in the darkest days of the year at that, is an excellent example of well-rewarded patience.

Please note that 'sow outside' means in a cold-frame that is unheated and which can be opened to allow frost to penetrate.

Plant name	Problem	Solution
Aconitum	Dormancy	Sow in autumn outside or chill for forty days before sowing in spring.
Actaea	Dormancy	As above. Berries are *poisonous*.
Alstroemeria	Dormancy, hard seed coat	Soak for twenty-four hours. Sow in individual pots. Require warmth, then cold. Sow in heat when ripe, then chill for twenty days, then return to heat. Process works in spring as well.
Anemone	Dormancy	Sow in autumn outside or chill for forty days before sowing in spring.
Anemonopsis macrophylla	Lime hater	Sow in spring in lime-free compost.
Anthyllis	Hard seed coat	Soak overnight in water that starts just below boiling.
Aquilegia (species only, not strains)	Dormancy	Sow in autumn or chill for twenty days before spring sowing.

Plant name	Problem	Solution
Armeria	Hard seed coat	Soak overnight in water that starts just below boiling.
Astilbe	Requires light and high humidity	Sow on surface, do not cover with compost. Wrap in clingfilm until first seedlings emerge. Treat for damping-off.
Astrantia	Dormancy	Sow in autumn outside or chill for thirty-five days before spring sowing.
Baptisia australis	Hard seed coat	Chip, or abrade between sheets of sandpaper, then soak in water for twenty-four hours.
Bergenia	Dormancy	Sow in autumn or not at all.
Clintonia	Lime hater	Sow in peat-based, lime-free compost.
Codonopsis	Not a lime hater, but germinates badly in lime	As above.
Convallaria majalis	Double domancy	Lily-of-the-valley. Treat as for Smilacina, q.v.
Cyananthus	Small seeds	Do not cover with compost.
Cypripedium	Orchid (hardy)	Don't bother. Needs laboratory treatment.
Dicentra	Dormancy	Sow in autumn or chill for twenty days before spring sowing.
Disporum	Dormancy. Lime hater	Sow in peaty compost in autumn or chill for thirty days before spring sowing.
Eccremocarpus	Requires light	Do not cover with compost.
Eryngium	Dormancy	Sow in autumn or chill for twenty days before spring sowing. Sometimes acceptable results without chilling.
Euphorbia (cold country species only)	Dormancy. Resistant seed coat	Sow in autumn or chill for fourteen days before spring sowing. Soak in water $\frac{1}{2}$ day before sowing. Warm temperate spp: sow in spring, no chilling, no soaking necessary.
Foeniculum	Dislikes root damage	Sow where it is to grow, then thin.
Gentiana (European)	Dormancy	Sow in autumn or chill for eighty days before spring sowing.
Gentiana (Asiatic)	Dormancy; lime haters	As above, but lime-free compost and watering.
Geranium	Seed-coat inhibitors; dormant embryo	Sow in autumn. Chilling for twenty–forty days may produce limited germination in spring. Occasionally there is an atypical massive germination from untreated spring sowings.
Glaucium	Tap-rooted	Sow where they are to grow. Subsequently allow to self-seed, then thin.

Plant name	Problem	Solution
Gunnera	Light-induced dormancy	Sow on peaty compost. Do not cover, but keep dark. *Some* light is necessary, but bright daylight has instant 'trigger' effect.
Helleborus	Dormancy	Sow in autumn outside and be prepared to wait. Some people are sensitive to seeds and hands may blister badly.
Hemerocallis	Partial dormancy	Sow outside in autumn. Spring sowings give reasonable results without chilling, but thirty-day chill doubles germination rate.
Incarvillea	Require light?	Sow in autumn outside. The author has always failed with spring sowings and remains mystified.
Iris	Dormancy	Sow in autumn outdoors. May take from four months to two years.
Lathyrus	Hard seed coat	Chip seeds or abrade between sheets of sandpaper.
Libertia	Require light	Sow in autumn broadcast, or sow in spring indoors, not covering with compost.
Lupin	Hard seed coat	Chip, abrade, or soak seeds. For rare strains, pre-germinate on blotting-paper, then pot up individually.
Lychnis	Impermeable seed coat. Dormancy	Sow in autumn or chill for fourteen days before abrading or soaking before spring sowing.
Meconopsis	The idea that they are difficult is handed down. Do require light, however	Break the cycle of legend by sowing in spring. Split seed and sow half outside in autumn if you are dubious. Do not cover with compost.
Papaver orientale	Requires light	Do not cover with compost.
Papaver; other spp.	No problem unless deeply covered	
Penstemon	(Dormancy)	The author has never found penstemons to present problems of dormancy, although authorities claim they exist.
Polygonatum	Dormancy	Sow in autumn or chill for twenty days before spring sowing.
Primula	Low viability Light required	The author has never experienced the least difficulty with seed of *Primula* spp. provided that the seed is fresh or has been stored cold. Do not cover with compost (includes polyanthus).
Pulsatilla	Dormancy; low viability of some seeds; dormancy in others	Sow in autumn, nose down, tail in air. Spring sowing: chill for twenty days, then sow with tails removed.

Plant name	Problem	Solution
Ranunculus	As above	Sow outside in autumn if at all possible, otherwise chill for twenty-eight days before spring sowing. May take two years—or may never emerge at all. Whole family Ranunculaceae is problematical and best sown in autumn.
Roscoea	Dormancy	Sow in autumn outside, or chill for twenty days before spring sowing.
Sedum	As above	As above.
Smilacina	Double dormancy	Chill for ninety days, then put in warmth for ninety days. Chill again for ninety days, then bring nto warmth for germination.
Trillium	As above	As above. Peaty compost, patience and consistent moisture are needed.
Trollius	Dormancy	Sow in autumn or chill for twenty days before spring sowing.

Bulb List

The following is a list of bulbs that can be grown from seed. It includes many that will need the protection of an unheated greenhouse, alpine house, or frame. It is not comprehensive, but should be enough to whet the appetite of those who have not tried bulbs from seed, and it might give some extra ideas to those who have. Unless otherwise stated, all should be sown as soon as the seed is ripe. Seed received from distant sources in the spring should be chilled if it is not too late and as long as the seed is not of tender species. Otherwise, it cannot be expected to germinate without delay of at least a year.

Plant name	Flower colour and size	Flowering time	Hardiness and general comments	Germination
Albuca humilis	White with green stripe, 4in (10cm)	Late spring	Slightly tender	
Allium species	Many colours and sizes	Spring and summer	Alliums—onions—are often extremely ornamental. In very cold places, including NE America, alliums should be protected in winter.	They are easy to germinate in the open frame.
Anemone blanda	Red, pink, blue, white, 4in (10cm)	Spring	Part shade. Not dry in summer	
Anemone biflora	Bright red, 3in (7.5cm)	Spring		Bulb frame. Germinate in greenhouse
Anthericum liliago	White, 2ft (60cm) (St. Bernard's lily)	Spring	Easy from seed, but transplant bulbs with care. Likes moisture and rich soil.	
Camassia species	Blue or white, 2¼ft (75cm)	Summer	Cool spots with plenty of moisture. Easy from abundantly-produced seed.	

Species	Description	Flowering	Soil/Site	Notes
Cardiocrinum giganteum	Large white lilies on stem up to 10ft (3m)	Summer	Cool, peaty place.	The giant Himalayan lily is utterly gorgeous, but its bulbs command a fearsome price. Very easy indeed from seed, which should be sown every year, as it can be seven years from seed to flowering, after which the bulbs die and leave offsets which take four or five years to flower.
Colchicum	Easily-grown autumn flowering sp. are pink, purple or white before leaves. More difficult spring-flowering sp. are lilac or white—one is yellow			All are easy from seed which *must* be sown when just ripened.
Crocosmia masonorum	Orange, 2ft (60cm)	Late summer and autumn	Slightly tender. Grow in large groups in sun for late colour	
Crocus species	Many different	Spring, some in autumn		Easy from seed if sown as soon as ripe. Germination reduced by storage
Cyclamen species	Mostly pink, red, white, mauve	Almost all year round		Sow while still sticky from the pod. Never allow pots to dry out. Transplant after two years. Seed of hardy *Cyclamen* spp. may reach you from commercial or other sources after it has gone dormant. This dormancy is very difficult to break and it may be the best counsel to suggest that the seed be sown and put into a cold frame for what is likely to be a period of two years or more. Alternatively, the following may be tried. Place moist kitchen paper in inverted lid from a jar of instant coffee. Place seeds on the paper. Wrap the whole in clingfilm and cover with piece of hardboard to keep out the light. Place on a warm, but not sunny windowsill. Inspect every week until germination begins, and prick off each seed as it shoots.
Erythronium species	Pink, yellow, white (Dog's tooth violets)	Spring	Woodsy, leafy soils. Not dry	*Erythronium* seed appears either to lose its viability in storage or to go into profound dormancy, or both. It is easy if sown as soon as ripe or a little after, but the pots of seedlings must never be allowed to become dry.

Plant name	Flower colour and size	Flowering time	Hardiness and general comments	Germination
Eranthis hyemalis	Yellow (Winter Aconite)	Early spring	Easy. Naturalizes in well-drained woodland	
Freesia				Seeds of the varieties of this most fragrant of flowers germinate at temperatures of around 18°C. They should be chipped with a knife like sweet pea seeds, as the seed coats are hard and impermeable. Sow thinly in deep pots. Plants will need daily watering; dryness is fatal. Do not allow to fall below 7°C or flowers will not be formed. Successional sowings give staggered flowering. Ventilate well.
Fritillaria species			A very large genus	Most species are quite easy to germinate. Growing-on varies from very easy to near-impossible.
Galanthus sp.	White and green (snow-drops)	Autumn, winter, and early spring	Easily divided 'in the green' but additional sp. are easy from seed to give you a long season of snowdrop flowers	
Galtonia candicans	White, 2–3ft (60–75cm)	Late summer	Easy from abundant seed sown in greenhouse. Slightly tender	
Iris species	Various	Spring and summer		All iris species will develop deep and prolonged dormancy if not sown as soon as ripe
Leucojum species	White, 8in–2ft (20–60cm) (Snowflakes)	Late spring, early autumn, late winter	Best in sunny places but not too hot and not dry. Not hardy in N Britain or NE United States and Canada	

Name	Description	Season	Notes	
Lilium species			Large genus	Most lilies germinate readily, even after storage, although it is still recommended that they be sown as soon as ripe. Some may appear to take much longer than others, but these tend to make a small bulb before a leaf appears and in fact can usually be planted out earlier than the others.
Moraea species	Large, brilliant orange, red, blue	Spring	Peacock moraeas are not hardy and require greenhouse treatment. Their great beauty demands their being grown, however. Easy from seed but four years to flowering	
Muscari	Generally blue (Grape hyacinths)	Spring	Easy from seed	
Narcissus species	Very large genus	Spring, *N. serotinus* in autumn	Most are easy from seed in unheated frame	
Nerine bowdenii	Pink, 10in—2ft (25–60cm)	Autumn	A little tender. Sow fleshy seeds immediately the pods split. Germination extremely fast. Do not cover seeds	
Nomocharis species	Lily relatives of great beauty. Pink, white, fringed, 2½–3½ft (75–105cm)	Summer	Require cool, moist, peaty conditions. Not suited at all to hot summers	Germinate with ease but hate disturbance. Sow thinly and plant whole potful after two years.
Ornithogalum species	White, green markings, 6in–3ft (15cm–1m)	Spring and summer	Many species, all easy from seed	
Paradisea liliastrum	White, scented, 1–2ft (30–60cm) (St. Bruno's lily)	Summer	Easy from seed	

Plant name	Flower colour and size	Flowering time	Hardiness and general comments	Germination
Rhodohypoxis sp.	White, red, pink, 1–2in (2.5–5cm)	Long succession of flowers from spring to autumn	Slightly tender. Must not dry out. Easy from seed and will self-sow if happy	
Scilla sp.	Pink, blue, white, mauve	Spring, summer, autumn flowering species	Easy from seed. S. African sp. are tender but resent winter wet more than cold	
Sparaxis mixed hybrids	Several colours, 6in (15cm) (Harlequin flower)	Late spring	Sow in greenhouse. Tender	
Tigridia pavonia	Red, orange, white, or yellow, spotted at centre, very large, spectacular, 18in (50cm)	Late summer to early autumn	Tender in N Britain and N America. Lift and store for winter. May flower in same year as sown.	
Trillium species	Flower parts in threes, white, pink, dark red, 3in–1ft (7.5–30cm)	Spring to early summer	Cool, peaty, woodland conditions. Seed must be sown perfectly fresh.	
Tulipa species	Large genus		Sow as soon as ripe but even so be prepared for up to five years to flowering.	
Watsonia hybrids	Mostly orangey pinks and reds, 2–3ft (60–90cm)	Summer	Easy from seed, even if it has been stored. Rather tender and do not like damp winters	

Some Sources of Seed

Chiltern Seeds
Bortree Stile
Ulverston
Cumbria LA12 7PB

Thompson & Morgan Limited
Ipswich
Suffolk

Unwins Seeds Limited
Histon
Cambridge CB4 4LE

S. E. Marshall & Co. Ltd.
Wisbech
Cambridgeshire. PE13 2RF

Jack Drake
Inshriach Alpine Plant Nursery
Aviemore
Inverness-shire

Phoenix Seeds
P.O. Box 9
Stanley
Tasmania 7331

Eden Seeds
The Finch Family
MS 316
Gympie
Queensland 4570

Ms Lindy Emmett
M.S. 1197
Cooloolabin
Via Nambour
Queensland 4560

Speciality Seeds
P.O. Box 34
Hawksburn
Victoria 3142

The Country Garden
Route 2, Box 455A
Crivitz,
Wisconsin 54114

J. L. Hudson, Seedsman
P.O. Box 1058
Redwood City
California 94064

Maver Rare Perennials
Route 2, Box 265 B
Asheville
North Carolina 28805

Geo. W. Park Seed Company
Greenwood
South Carolina 29647

Societies

(access to seed lists implies membership)

The Royal Horticultural Society
Vincent Square
London SW1P 2PE

The Alpine Garden Society
Lye End Link
St. John's
Woking
Surrey

The American Rock Garden Society
15 Fairmead Road
Darien
Connecticut 06820

The Scottish Rock Garden Club
21 Merchiston Park
Edinburgh EH10 4PW

References

Atwater, B. R. (1980). *Seed Sci. & Technol.* 8. 523–573. Germination, dormancy and morphology of the seeds of herbaceous ornamental plants.

Schopmeyer, C. S. (1974). Seeds of Woody Plants in the United States. *Agriculture Handbook* 450. U.S. Department of Agriculture (Forest Service). Washington.

Huxley, A. *Plant and Planet*. Allen Lane. 1974.

Acknowledgments

I would like to thank Douglas Bowden of Ulverston, Cumbria and Margaret Waddy of Cambridge for their kind assistance, and to acknowledge the contribution made by Julian Holland, designer.

Index